poem-a-day

365 Poems for Every Occasion

poem-a-day

365 Poems for Every Occasion

THE ACADEMY OF AMERICAN POETS
ABRAMS IMAGE, NEW YORK

Editor: Tamar Brazis
Designer: Devin Grosz
Production Manager: Anet Sirna-Bruder

Library of Congress Control Number: 2014959312

ISBN: 978-1-4197-1799-4

Compilation copyright © 2015 The Academy of American Poets

Printed and bound in the United States

10 9 8 7 6 5 4 3 2

Abrams Image books are available at special discounts when
purchased in quantity for premiums and promotions as well
as fundraising or educational use. Special editions can also
be created to specification. For details, contact specialsales@
abramsbooks.com or the address below.

ABRAMS The Art of Books
115 West 18th Street, New York, NY 10011
abramsbooks.com

Contents

Introduction

A poem is an experience. It puts language under pressure. Something unexpected happens in words—something mysterious—that I cannot quite explain, and suddenly my perception is heightened, my viewpoint altered (challenged, confirmed), and my world realigned—sometimes in a small quotidian way, sometimes in a larger, more enduring one. I read to be disturbed, confronted, consoled. I read to be reawakened. Sometimes I know what I am looking for—a poem for a holiday, a special occasion, to help me name my feelings (for myself, for others)—but other times I do not know what I am seeking until I find it. I did not recognize that I was hungry, spiritually speaking, until I sat down and ate. These are the most thrilling acts of reading. I experience the poem in my pulse and find myself launched into the unknown, a place I somehow recognize.

Our feelings are outsize—each of us has a great abundance, a deep well of grief within him (or her)—and poetry plumbs the depths of our inner and outer lives. It estranges the familiar world. On any given day, every person plays a variety of recognizable social roles, fulfills many defined functions, and also moves through a cloud of unknowing. In one sense, we know what we are supposed to do—we manage our tasks, enact our roles—but in another sense we have no idea where we are going or what is going to happen to us. Poetry is a reminder of our mortality, the fragility of existence; it is an intervention in the prose of life. It is at once private (it speaks to our inner subjective lives) and social (it comes to us through the circuit of language, which belongs to everyone). Robert Frost called a poem "a momentary stay against confusion."

The Academy of American Poets has been staging its own quiet intervention, its own stay against confusion, with its Poem-a-Day series, which provides 365 poems a year—weekday contemporaries, weekend classics. This anthology is a result of that series' runaway popularity. It gives us a year full of lyrics. It is arranged by month and theme, and thus cycles through the seasons. Beginning in January, the collection winds through an allegorical year—with its holidays and its transitions, both human and natural. It concludes at the end of December with the gift of friendship. I recommend using it as a daily companion. Read one poem per day over the course of a year and you will find yourself befriended by poetry.

Poetry is a means of transport, taking us back in time, carrying us forward, lifting us up. It is a mode of thinking, a method of flight, an act of concentrated attention. It associates rapidly and sings us into being. Whoever touches this book will touch many men, many women, and will have many encounters, a whole range of experiences—some solitary, some communal. Poetry is a form of necessary speech. It is, as Wallace Stevens called it, "one of the enlargements of life."

—EDWARD HIRSCH,
   Chancellor of the Academy of American Poets (2008–2014)

January

CARL ADAMSHICK
(1969–)

New year's morning

A low, quiet music is playing—
distorted trumpet, torn bass line,
white windows. My palms
are two speakers the size
of pool-hall coasters.
I lay them on the dark table
for you to repair.

JIMMY SANTIAGO BACA
(1952–)

This Day

I feel foolish,
    like those silly robins jumping on the ditch boughs
    when I run by them.
        Those robins do not have the grand style of the red-tailed hawk,
        no design, no dream, just robins acting stupid.
They've never smoked cigarettes, drank whiskey, consumed drugs
as I have.
    In their mindless
    fluttering about
    filled with nonsense,
      they tell me how they
         love the Great Spirit,
    scold me not to be self-pitying,
    to open my life
    and make this day a bough on a tree
    leaning over eternity, where eternity flows forward
    and with day the river runs
      carrying all that falls in it.
    Be happy Jimmy, they chirp,
    Jimmy, be silly, make this day a tree
    leaning over the river eternity
    and fuss about in its branches.

TRACY K. SMITH
(1972–)

The Soul

The voice is clean. Has heft. Like stones
Dropped in still water, or tossed
One after the other at a low wall.
Chipping away at what pushes back.
Not always making a dent, but keeping at it.
And the silence around it is a door
Punched through with light. A garment
That attests to breasts, the privacy
Between thighs. The body is what we lean toward,
Tensing as it darts, dancing away.
But it's the voice that enters us. Even
Saying nothing. Even saying nothing
Over and over absently to itself.

D. H. LAWRENCE
(1885–1930)

Moonrise

And who has seen the moon, who has not seen
Her rise from out the chamber of the deep,
Flushed and grand and naked, as from the chamber
Of finished bridegroom, seen her rise and throw
Confession of delight upon the wave,
Littering the waves with her own superscription
Of bliss, till all her lambent beauty shakes towards us
Spread out and known at last, and we are sure
That beauty is a thing beyond the grave,
That perfect, bright experience never falls
To nothingness, and time will dim the moon
Sooner than our full consummation here
In this odd life will tarnish or pass away.

SARA TEASDALE
(1884–1933)

A Winter Bluejay

Crisply the bright snow whispered,
Crunching beneath our feet;
Behind us as we walked along the parkway,
Our shadows danced,
Fantastic shapes in vivid blue.
Across the lake the skaters
Flew to and fro,
With sharp turns weaving
A frail invisible net.
In ecstasy the earth
Drank the silver sunlight;
In ecstasy the skaters
Drank the wine of speed;
In ecstasy we laughed
Drinking the wine of love.
Had not the music of our joy
Sounded its highest note?
But no,
For suddenly, with lifted eyes you said,
"Oh look!"
There, on the black bough of a snow flecked maple,
Fearless and gay as our love,
A bluejay cocked his crest!
Oh who can tell the range of joy
Or set the bounds of beauty?

CAMILLE T. DUNGY
(1972–)

Survival

The body winnows. The body tills. The body knows
sow's feet, sow gut, night harvested kale. The body knows
to sleep through welted dreams, to wake
before the night succumbs to morning.

Wheat, wheat, tobacco, corn: the body knows.

No stopping. No sinking down. Like a branch
floats on water, the body does not go under.
Like a tree seeded among dark rocks, the body
leans where it must. Or fails.

RUTH STONE
(1915–2011)

The Cabbage

You have rented an apartment.
You come to this enclosure with physical relief,
your heavy body climbing the stairs in the dark,
the hall bulb burned out, the landlord
of Greek extraction and possibly a fatalist.
In the apartment leaning against one wall,
your daughter's painting of a large frilled cabbage
against a dark sky with pinpoints of stars.
The eager vegetable, opening itself
as if to eat the air, or speak in cabbage
language of the meanings within meanings;
while the points of stars hide their massive
violence in the dark upper half of the painting.
You can live with this.

NOELLE KOCOT
(1969–)

On Being an Artist

Saturn seems habitual,
The way it rages in the sky
When we're not looking.
On this note, the trees still sing
To me, and I long for this
Mottled world. Patterns
Of the lamplight on this leather,
The sun, listening.
My brother, my sister,
I was born to tell you certain
Things, even if no one
Really listens. Give it back
To me, as the bird takes up
The whole sky, ruined with
Nightfall. If I can remember
The words in the storm,
I will be well enough to sit
Here with you a little while.

DENIS JOHNSON
(1949–)

Man Walking to Work

The dawn is a quality laid across
the freeway like the visible
memory of the ocean that kept all this
a secret for a hundred million years.
I am not moving and I am not standing still.
I am only something the wind strikes and clears,
and I feel myself fade like the sky,
the whole of Ohio a mirror gone blank.
My jacket keeps me. My zipper
bangs on my guitar. Lord God help me
out by the lake after the shift at Frigidaire
when I stop laughing and taste how wet the beer
is in my mouth, suddenly recognizing the true
wedding of passage and arrival I am invited to.

ROBINSON JEFFERS
(1887–1962)

Wonder and Joy

The things that one grows tired of—O, be sure
They are only foolish artificial things!
Can a bird ever tire of having wings?
And I, so long as life and sense endure,
(Or brief be they!) shall nevermore inure
My heart to the recurrence of the springs,
Of the gray dawns, the gracious evenings,
The infinite wheeling stars. A wonder pure
Must ever well within me to behold
Venus decline; or great Orion, whose belt
Is studded with three nails of burning gold,
Ascend the winter heaven. Who never felt
This wondering joy may yet be good or great:
But envy him not: he is not fortunate.

At the Very Beginning

When I named you I was on the verge
of a discovery, I was accumulating

data, my condition was that of a person
sitting late at night in a yellowing kitchen

over steeping tea mumbling
as his wife remotely does the laundry.

My condition was that of a mathematician
who cannot put the names to colors,

who, confusing speaking and addition,
identifies with confidence the rain

soaked broad trunked redwood tree (whose
scent releases all of winter) saying as he passes *one*

NAOMI SHIHAB NYE
(1952–)

Burning the Old Year

Letters swallow themselves in seconds.
Notes friends tied to the doorknob,
transparent scarlet paper,
sizzle like moth wings,
marry the air.

So much of any year is flammable,
lists of vegetables, partial poems.
Orange swirling flame of days,
so little is a stone.

Where there was something and suddenly isn't,
an absence shouts, celebrates, leaves a space.
I begin again with the smallest numbers.

Quick dance, shuffle of losses and leaves,
only the things I didn't do
crackle after the blazing dies.

ADAM CLAY
(1978–)

Our Daily Becoming

Like animals moving daily
through the same open field,
it should be easier to distinguish
light from dark, fabrications

from memory, rain on a sliver
of grass from dew appearing
overnight. In these moments
of desperation, a sentence

serves as a halo, the moon
hidden so the stars eclipse
our daily becoming. You think
it should be easier to define

one's path, but with the clouds
gathering around our feet,
there's no sense in retracing
where we've been or where

your tired body will carry you.
Eventually the birds become
confused and inevitable. Even our
infinite knowledge of the forecast

might make us more vulnerable
than we would be in drawn-out
ignorance. To the sun
all weeds eventually rise up.

ALICE NOTLEY
(1945-   )

Individual Time

I'm calling out from pictures to your vision creating it
turn right, that dream building cutglass window in door.
Automatically inside their apartment, you don't have
to get there. This is before the lost sacred corpus vision,
someone says Look at my author photo. I
don't really want to I'm turning to defiant metal
not a dream part, can you see it where the movement of
images turns back towards me I want a
different, how I'm portrayed because you can't
see me, visage. Look at me please. The soul is so thick
larger than the portrait what you'd call madonnaesque,
and then there was more hoax a view as I am
the rose here. And you never wanted to be that, did I?
I was waiting to see what I would be. Blackness
eats you but your soul eats it without your knowing that
figure, because it is causing your appearance to the world.
They arrange me in clothes of Easter, or of
the first day of classes, but I'm projecting pigment
cracked gold on fire, thinking braver thoughts.
It takes courage to get to the ancient altar
of the moment where I create individual time.
The picture body untremblingly stares large-eyed
I also create the tablets of exponential seeing: it brightens
all around it, as I'm the apparatus of what there is to be;
and I am making it, my time visibly becoming me.

KATIE FORD
(1975–)

Snow at Night

I prefer it even to love,
alone and without ghost
it falls a hard weather,
a withdrawing room
that revives me to stolen daylight
in which I feel no wish
to brush a gleaming finish
over the sheen-broken glass
I've arranged and rearranged
as apprentice of mosaics
who will not be taught but asks
to be left alone with the brittle year
so carnivorous of all I'd made.
But the snow I love covers
my beasts and seas,
my ferns and spines
worn through and through.
I will change your life, it says,
to which I say *please*.

MAY SWENSON
(1913–1989)

Question

Body my house
my horse my hound
what will I do
when you are fallen

Where will I sleep
How will I ride
What will I hunt

Where can I go
without my mount
all eager and quick
How will I know
in thicket ahead
is danger or treasure
when Body my good
bright dog is dead

How will it be
to lie in the sky
without roof or door
and wind for an eye

With cloud for shift
how will I hide?

WILLIAM STAFFORD
(1914–1993)

Once in the 40s

We were alone one night on a long
road in Montana. This was in winter, a big
night, far to the stars. We had hitched,
my wife and I, and left our ride at
a crossing to go on. Tired and cold—but
brave—we trudged along. This, we said,
was our life, watched over, allowed to go
where we wanted. We said we'd come back some time
when we got rich. We'd leave the others and find
a night like this, whatever we had to give,
and no matter how far, to be so happy again.

HARRYETTE MULLEN
(1953–)

Muse & Drudge
[just as I am I come]

just as I am I come
knee bent and body bowed
this here's sorrow's home
my body's southern song

cram all you can
into jelly jam
preserve a feeling
keep it sweet

so beautiful it was
presumptuous to alter
the shape of my pleasure
in doing or making

proceed with abandon
finding yourself where you are
and who you're playing for
what stray companion

EDGAR ALLAN POE
(1809–1849)

A Dream Within a Dream

Take this kiss upon the brow!
And, in parting from you now,
Thus much let me avow—
You are not wrong, who deem
That my days have been a dream;
Yet if Hope has flown away
In a night, or in a day,
In a vision, or in none,
Is it therefore the less *gone*?
All that we see or seem
Is but a dream within a dream.

I stand amid the roar
Of a surf-tormented shore,
And I hold within my hand
Grains of the golden sand—
How few! yet how they creep
Through my fingers to the deep,
While I weep—while I weep!
O God! can I not grasp
Them with a tighter clasp?
O God! can I not save
One from the pitiless wave?
Is *all* that we see or seem
But a dream within a dream?

ROGER REEVES
(1980–)

Before Diagnosis

The lake is dead for a second time
this January. And no matter
how many geese lay their warm breasts
against the ice or fly across
its hard chest, it doesn't break,
or sink, or open up and swallow them.
The ice is frozen water.
There is no metaphor for exile.
Even if these trees continue to shake
the crows from their branches,
my sister is still farther away from her mind
than we are from each other,
sitting on opposite ends of a park bench
waiting for evening to swallow us whole.
In the last moments of a depressive, a sun.
In the last moments of a sun, my sister
says a man is chasing a goose through the snow.

HELEN HUNT JACKSON
(1830–1885)

January

O Winter! frozen pulse and heart of fire,
What loss is theirs who from thy kingdom turn
Dismayed, and think thy snow a sculptured urn
Of death! Far sooner in midsummer tire
The streams than under ice. June could not hire
Her roses to forego the strength they learn
In sleeping on thy breast. No fires can burn
The bridges thou dost lay where men desire
In vain to build.
           O Heart, when Love's sun goes
To northward, and the sounds of singing cease,
Keep warm by inner fires, and rest in peace.
Sleep on content, as sleeps the patient rose.
Walk boldly on the white untrodden snows,
The winter is the winter's own release.

Room Tone

Wrestling that old beauty
"Body and Soul"
To the ground

The genus award for epochal comes besotted
Complicity follows like caramel on a sponge mop
Child-bearing babies on stilts

I dreamed you were felled by an unspecified illness
In yours I was rowing a leaky boat, even though
The motor was foolproof and bore hairs

Taken up with travel and foreign visitors
An intimacy implied in big block letters leans
Beside its planar incandescent surrogate

I tend backward haughtily through froth
Abandoned sweetness meaning torpor
Behind gorgeous intervals of removal and need

An alligator in every pot
Keeping company doesn't count
Dame Kind adjusts her ribbon frills

Give life a shot
Circular breath redemption
At the Door of the Wolf

You heard me

Excelsior

Who has gone farthest? for I would go farther,
And who has been just? for I would be the most just person of the earth,
And who most cautious? for I would be more cautious,
And who has been happiest? O I think it is I—I think no one was ever
 happier than I,
And who has lavish'd all? for I lavish constantly the best I have,
And who proudest? for I think I have reason to be the proudest son
 alive—for I am the son of the brawny and tall-topt city,
And who has been bold and true? for I would be the boldest and truest
 being of the universe,
And who benevolent? for I would show more benevolence than all the
 rest,
And who has receiv'd the love of the most friends? for I know what it is to
 receive the passionate love of many friends,
And who possesses a perfect and enamour'd body? for I do not believe any
 one possesses a more perfect or enamour'd body than mine,
And who thinks the amplest thoughts? for I would surround those
 thoughts,
And who has made hymns fit for the earth? for I am mad with devouring
 ecstasy to make joyous hymns for the whole earth.

BETTY ADCOCK
(1938–)

January

Dusk and snow this hour
in argument have settled
nothing. Light persists,
and darkness. If a star
shines now, that shine is
swallowed and given back
doubled, grounded bright.
The timid angels flailed
by passing children lift
in a whitening wind
toward night. What plays
beyond the window plays
as water might, all parts
making cold digress.
Beneath iced bush and eave,
the small banked fires of birds
at rest lend absences
to seeming absence. Truth
is, nothing at all is missing.
Wind hisses and one shadow
sways where a window's lampglow
has added something. The rest
is dark and light together tolled
against the boundary-riven
houses. Against our lives,
the stunning wholeness of the world.

LANGSTON HUGHES
(1902–1967)

Dreams

Hold fast to dreams
For if dreams die
Life is a broken-winged bird
That cannot fly.

Hold fast to dreams
For when dreams go
Life is a barren field
Frozen with snow.

LIA PURPURA
(1964–)

Gone

It's that, when I'm gone,
(and right off this is tricky)
I won't be worried
about being gone.
I won't be here
to miss anything.
I want now, sure,
all I've been gathering
since I was born,
but later
when I no longer have it,
(which might be
a state everlasting, who knows?)
this moment right now
(stand closer, love,
you can't be too close),
is not a thing I'll know to miss.
I doubt I'll miss it.
I can't get over this.

RAINER MARIA RILKE
(1875–1926)

Archaic Torso of Apollo

We cannot know his legendary head
with eyes like ripening fruit. And yet his torso
is still suffused with brilliance from inside,
like a lamp, in which his gaze, now turned to low,

gleams in all its power. Otherwise
the curved breast could not dazzle you so, nor could
a smile run through the placid hips and thighs
to that dark center where procreation flared.

Otherwise this stone would seem defaced
beneath the translucent cascade of the shoulders
and would not glisten like a wild beast's fur:

would not, from all the borders of itself,
burst like a star: for here there is no place
that does not see you. You must change your life.

MELISSA BRODER
(1982–)

Wide Sigh

I thought that there were two
The good voice
And my voice

I thought the good voice was buried
And I would have to go
Under my voice
Which is glittery and cold
To get there

Then I heard them
A drumbeat and hawks
Also snakes
Many wild voices

Heartbeats
Big beats
One beat
All over

Do you hear it?
I hear it now
Speeding up
Taking me up

The Year's Awakening

How do you know that the pilgrim track
Along the belting zodiac
Swept by the sun in his seeming rounds
Is traced by now to the Fishes' bounds
And into the Ram, when weeks of cloud
Have wrapt the sky in a clammy shroud,
And never as yet a tinct of spring
Has shown in the Earth's apparelling;
   O vespering bird, how do you know,
     How do you know?

How do you know, deep underground,
Hid in your bed from sight and sound,
Without a turn in temperature,
With weather life can scarce endure,
That light has won a fraction's strength,
And day put on some moments' length,
Whereof in merest rote will come,
Weeks hence, mild airs that do not numb;
   O crocus root, how do you know,
     How do you know?

DORA MALECH
(1981–)

Each year

I snap the twig to try to trap
the springing and I relearn the same lesson.
You cannot make a keepsake of this season.
Your heart's not the source of that sort of sap,
lacks what it takes to fuel, rejects the graft,
though for a moment it's your guilty fist
that's flowering. You're no good host to this
extremity that points now, broken, back at
the dirt as if to ask *are we there yet.*
You flatter this small turn tip of a larger
book of matches that can't refuse its end,
re-fuse itself, un-flare. Sure. Now forget again.
Here's a new green vein, another
clutch to take, give, a handful of seconds.

How to Love

After stepping into the world again,
there is that question of how to love,
how to bundle yourself against the frosted morning —
the crunch of icy grass underfoot, the scrape
of cold wipers along the windshield —
and convert time into distance.

What song to sing down an empty road
as you begin your morning commute?
And is there enough in you to see, really see,
the three wild turkeys crossing the street
with their featherless heads and stilt-like legs
in search of a morning meal? Nothing to do
but hunker down, wait for them to safely cross.

As they amble away, you wonder if they want
to be startled back into this world. Maybe you do, too,
waiting for all this to give way to love itself,
to look into the eyes of another and feel something —
the pleasure of a new lover in the unbroken night,
your wings folded around him, on the other side
of this ragged January, as if a long sleep has ended.

February

After Making Love
We Hear Footsteps

For I can snore like a bullhorn
or play loud music
or sit up talking with any reasonably sober Irishman
and Fergus will only sink deeper
into his dreamless sleep, which goes by all in one flash,
but let there be that heavy breathing
or a stifled come-cry anywhere in the house
and he will wrench himself awake
and make for it on the run—as now, we lie together,
after making love, quiet, touching along the length of our bodies,
familiar touch of the long-married,
and he appears—in his baseball pajamas, it happens,
the neck opening so small he has to screw them on—
and flops down between us and hugs us and snuggles himself to sleep,
his face gleaming with satisfaction at being this very child.

In the half darkness we look at each other
and smile
and touch arms across this little, startlingly muscled body—
this one whom habit of memory propels to the ground of his making,
sleeper only the mortal sounds can sing awake,
this blessing love gives again into our arms.

LUCILLE CLIFTON
(1936–2010)

blessing the boats

(at St. Mary's)

may the tide
that is entering even now
the lip of our understanding
carry you out
beyond the face of fear
may you kiss
the wind then turn from it
certain that it will
love your back   may you
open your eyes to water
water waving forever
and may you in your innocence
sail through this to that

ANNIE FINCH
(1956–)

Love in the Morning

Morning's a new bird
stirring against me
out of a quiet nest,
coming to flight—

quick-changing,
slow-nodding,
breath-filling body,

life-holding,
waiting,
clean as clear water,

warmth-given,
fire-driven
kindling companion,

mystery and mountain,
dark-rooted,
earth-anchored.

EMILY DICKINSON
(1830–1886)

Wild Nights—
Wild Nights! (249)

Wild Nights—Wild Nights!
Were I with thee
Wild Nights should be
Our luxury!

Futile—the Winds—
To a Heart in port—
Done with the Compass—
Done with the Chart!

Rowing in Eden—
Ah, the Sea!
Might I but moor—Tonight—
In Thee!

JONATHAN WELLS
(1954–)

Love's Body

Love gives all its reasons
as if they were terms for peace.
Love is this but not that
that but not this.
Love as it always was.

But there is no peace in the mountain
cleft where the fruit bats scatter
from the light.
There is no peace in the hollow when
the heat snuffs night's blue candle.

The outline of brown leaves on
the beach is the wind's body.

A crow is squawking at the sun
as if the screech itself is dawn.
Let me hear every perfect note.
How I loved that jasper morning.

PAIGE TAGGART
(1981–)

You Make Love Like
the Last Snow Leopard

You make love like the last
snow leopard. Time hunts your shadows.
Your grooves dip a real x of an arc.
I love your shadow. Its performance on the wall.

Your white hair flocked. It's old age that makes
you kill for food. You bring a long blank to
bed in, the weight draws out.

You need someone with skill for the excursion.
Ride through the reservoir of sour peaches.
Your name meanders through the grass. Tall
people are in the way. I crowd surf to get to you.

You spill me into the flood. Water rushes out your sides.

You make a mystery of playing political love.
I could kill for you. I'd bring you an eagle stuffed
with finches. Its pouch growing large and groaning
in your palm. A cliff of umbrellas and memory
shaping your every move.

MATTHEW ROHRER
(1970–)

Credo

I believe there is something else

entirely going on but no single
person can ever know it,
so we fall in love.

It could also be true that what we use
everyday to open cans was something
much nobler, that we'll never recognize.

I believe the woman sleeping beside me
doesn't care about what's going on
outside, and her body is warm
with trust
which is a great beginning.

ELIZABETH BISHOP
(1911–1979)

One Art

The art of losing isn't hard to master;
so many things seem filled with the intent
to be lost that their loss is no disaster.

Lose something every day. Accept the fluster
of lost door keys, the hour badly spent.
The art of losing isn't hard to master.

Then practice losing farther, losing faster:
places, and names, and where it was you meant
to travel. None of these will bring disaster.

I lost my mother's watch. And look! my last, or
next-to-last, of three loved houses went.
The art of losing isn't hard to master.

I lost two cities, lovely ones. And, vaster,
some realms I owned, two rivers, a continent.
I miss them, but it wasn't a disaster.

—Even losing you (the joking voice, a gesture
I love) I shan't have lied. It's evident
the art of losing's not too hard to master
though it may look like (*Write* it!) like disaster.

poem I wrote sitting across the table from you

if I had two nickels to rub together
I would rub them together

like a kid rubs sticks together
until friction made combustion

and they burned
a hole in my pocket

into which I would put my hand
and then my arm

and eventually my whole self—
I would fold myself

into the hole in my pocket and disappear
into the pocket of myself, or at least my pants

but before I did
like some ancient star

I'd grab your hand

AUDRE LORDE
(1934–1992)

The Black Unicorn

The black unicorn is greedy.
The black unicorn is impatient.
The black unicorn was mistaken
for a shadow
or symbol
and taken
through a cold country
where mist painted mockeries
of my fury.
It is not on her lap where the horn rests
but deep in her moonpit
growing.

The black unicorn is restless
the black unicorn is unrelenting
the black unicorn is not
free.

KHALED MATTAWA
(1964–)

Airporter

Yardley, Pennsylvania, an expensive dump
and the van seats shake their broken bones.

Duty-free liquor and cigarettes,
the refineries and the harbor's cranes.

The moon digs its way out of the dirt.
The branches of an evergreen sway.

She's nice
the woman you don't love.

She kisses you hard and often
holding your face in her big hands.

Q

May I master love, undo its luster
do in the thing that makes us lust?

May I speed through the body's sinew
to marrow? Or is toiling a part of

the gaining of trust? May I pare and narrow
your body down, and open it to my

cupidity's arrow? May I find my
response to body's unanswered call,

(if the want leaves you wanting, at all)?

NORMAN DUBIE
(1945–)

You

The sunlight passes through the window into the room
Where you are sewing a button to your blouse: outside
Water in the fountain rises
Toward a cloud. This plume of water is lighter
Now, for white shares of itself are falling back
Toward the ground.
This water does succeed, like us,
In nearing a perfect exhaustion,
Which is its origin. The water

Succeeds in leaving the ground but
It fails at its desire to reach a cloud. It pauses,
Falling back into its blue trough; of course,
Another climb is inevitable, and this loud, falling
Water is a figure for love, not loss, and

Still heavy with its desire to be the cloud.

PAUL LAURENCE DUNBAR
(1872–1906)

Invitation to Love

Come when the nights are bright with stars
   Or when the moon is mellow;
Come when the sun his golden bars
   Drops on the hay-field yellow.
Come in the twilight soft and gray,
Come in the night or come in the day,
Come, O Love, whene'er you may,
   And you are welcome, welcome.

You are sweet, O Love, dear Love,
You are soft as the nesting dove.
Come to my heart and bring it rest
As the bird flies home to its welcome nest.

Come when my heart is full of grief
   Or when my heart is merry;
Come with the falling of the leaf
   Or with the redd'ning cherry.
Come when the year's first blossom blows,
Come when the summer gleams and glows,
Come with the winter's drifting snows,
   And you are welcome, welcome.

DOROTHEA LASKY
(1978–)

The Wall Hanging
I Never Noticed

I never noticed before
How the red flowers hang from the blue branches
I never noticed before the light in this room
I never noticed the way the air is cool again
I never noticed anything but you
But you but you
So that I couldn't sleep
I never noticed what was anything but you
Until I noticed you
And could not help it
Until I noticed you I could not help it
Until you made the red flowers alive again
Until the blue branches
The lemons you loved, but also the way you loved me, too
Until all of this I never noticed you
But once I did
I never minded noticing
I never stopped noticing
Until I noticed you
I never stopped noticing
Until you, I never stopped

Black Boys Play
the Classics

The most popular "act" in
Penn Station
is the three black kids in ratty
sneakers & T-shirts playing
two violins and a cello—Brahms.
White men in business suits
have already dug into their pockets
as they pass and they toss in
a dollar or two without stopping.
Brown men in work-soiled khakis
stand with their mouths open,
arms crossed on their bellies
as if they themselves have always
wanted to attempt those bars.
One white boy, three, sits
cross-legged in front of his
idols—in ecstasy—
their slick, dark faces,
their thin, wiry arms,
who must begin to look
like angels!
Why does this trembling
pull us?
A: *Beneath the surface we are one.*
B: *Amazing! I did not think that they could speak this tongue.*

VICTORIA CHANG
(1970–)

Desire

A space must be maintained or desire ends.
—Anne Carson

The sun applies itself and bends, tries to debut
on my ankle, tries to copyright my body.
Because of you I let the sun iron my back until
it combusts. I let the waves swindle my body,
enter all of its cavities. I let the airplane in the
sky disappear, just as the white clothes on the
line become the wind. It is not space I desire,
but a dying, as crows might stalk the sky, bankrupt
air, content in their coming and going, content
in their similar blackness, in how their blackness
resembles every shadow; as clothes in a dryer in
a laundromat at 3 a.m. might finally stop
unclenching and accept their entanglement.

FRANK BIDART
(1939–)

Love Incarnate

(Dante, *Vita Nuova*)

To all those driven berserk or humanized by love
this is offered, for I need help
deciphering my dream.
When we love our lord is LOVE.

When I recall that at the fourth hour
of the night, watched by shining stars,
LOVE at last became incarnate,
the memory is horror.

In his hands smiling LOVE held my burning
heart, and in his arms, the body whose greeting
pierces my soul, now wrapped in bloodred, sleeping.

He made him wake. He ordered him to eat
my heart. He ate my burning heart. He ate it
submissively, as if afraid, as LOVE wept.

LI-YOUNG LEE
(1957–)

One Heart

Look at the birds. Even flying
is born

out of nothing. The first sky
is inside you, open

at either end of day.
The work of wings

was always freedom, fastening
one heart to every falling thing.

NICK FLYNN
(1960–)

forgetting something

Try this—close / your eyes. No, wait, when—if—we see each other /
again, the first thing we should do is close our eyes—no, / first we should
tie our hands to something / solid—bedpost, doorknob—otherwise they
(wild birds) / might startle us / awake. Are we forgetting something? What
about that / warehouse, the one beside the airport, that room / of black
boxes, a man in each box? If you / bring this one into the light he will not
stop / crying, if you show this one a photo of his son / his eyes go dead.
Turn up / the heat, turn up the song. First thing we should do / if we see
each other again is to make / a cage of our bodies—inside we can place /
whatever still shines.

W. H. AUDEN
(1907–1973)

The More Loving One

Looking up at the stars, I know quite well
That, for all they care, I can go to hell,
But on earth indifference is the least
We have to dread from man or beast.

How should we like it were stars to burn
With a passion for us we could not return?
If equal affection cannot be,
Let the more loving one be me.

Admirer as I think I am
Of stars that do not give a damn,
I cannot, now I see them, say
I missed one terribly all day.

Were all stars to disappear or die,
I should learn to look at an empty sky
And feel its total dark sublime,
Though this might take me a little time.

EDNA ST. VINCENT MILLAY
(1892–1952)

Love is Not All
(Sonnet XXX)

Love is not all: it is not meat nor drink
Nor slumber nor a roof against the rain;
Nor yet a floating spar to men that sink
And rise and sink and rise and sink again;
Love can not fill the thickened lung with breath,
Nor clean the blood, nor set the fractured bone;
Yet many a man is making friends with death
Even as I speak, for lack of love alone.
It well may be that in a difficult hour,
Pinned down by pain and moaning for release,
Or nagged by want past resolution's power,
I might be driven to sell your love for peace,
Or trade the memory of this night for food.
It well may be. I do not think I would.

DEAN YOUNG
(1955–)

Ash Ode

When I saw you ahead I ran two blocks
shouting your name then realizing it wasn't
you but some alarmed pretender, I went on
running, shouting now into the sky,
continuing your fame and luster. Since I've
been incinerated, I've oft returned to this thought,
that all things loved are pursued and never caught,
even as you slept beside me you were flying off.
At least what's never had can't be lost, the sieve
of self stuck with just some larger chunks, jawbone,
wedding ring, a single repeated dream,
a lullaby in every elegy, descriptions
of the sea written in the desert, your broken
umbrella, me claiming I could fix it.

JANE HIRSHFIELD
(1953–)

For What Binds Us

There are names for what binds us:
strong forces, weak forces.
Look around, you can see them:
the skin that forms in a half-empty cup,
nails rusting into the places they join,
joints dovetailed on their own weight.
The way things stay so solidly
wherever they've been set down—
and gravity, scientists say, is weak.

And see how the flesh grows back
across a wound, with a great vehemence,
more strong
than the simple, untested surface before.
There's a name for it on horses,
when it comes back darker and raised: proud flesh,

as all flesh
is proud of its wounds, wears them
as honors given out after battle,
small triumphs pinned to the chest—

And when two people have loved each other
see how it is like a
scar between their bodies,
stronger, darker, and proud;
how the black cord makes of them a single fabric
that nothing can tear or mend.

PATRICIA SMITH
(1955–)

They Romp with Wooly Canines

and spy whole lifetimes on the undersides of leaves.
Jazz intrudes, stank clogging that neat procession
of lush and flutter. His eyes, siphoned and dimming,
demand that he accept ardor as it is presented, with
its tear-splashed borders and stilted lists, romance
that is only on the agenda because hours do not stop.
Bless his sliver of soul. He's nabbed a sizzling matron
who grays as we watch, a thick-ankled New England
whoop, muscled to suffer his stifling missionary weight.
Earth-smudged behind the wheel of her pickup,
she hums a tune that rhymes dots of dinner trapped
in his beard with twilight. Is it still a collision course
if you must lie down to rest? Bless her as she tries
on his name for size and plucks hairs from her chin.
Bless him as he barrels toward yet another wife
who will someday realize, idly, that her only purpose
in this dwindling novella of his days is to someday
lower his heralded bulk, with little fanfare, into a grave.

CAKI WILKINSON
(1980–)

Fox

The yards grow ghosts. Between the limbs and wings,
bleached street-lit things, I'm best at moving on.
Hunt-heavy, gray, slunk overlow like so
much weight got in the way, my shape's the shape
of something missed, flash-pop or empty frame.
Though you could say I've made a game of this,
and though midtrickery it might be true,
when evening lingers in the key of leaving
my senses swoon. A synonym for stay,
I'm always coming back. I chew through traps.
I love whatever doesn't get too close.

MATTHEA HARVEY
(1973–)

Woman Lives in House Made of People

They were lonely. I was alone.
Out of those two sentences,

I made myself a home. My house sighs,
has a hundred heartbeats, dimpled

cupboards and a pink mouth for a mailbox.
There's always a tangle of legs in my bed.

O the walls have eyes, the baseboards
have toes. The decorative molding (rows of noses)

twitches and sniffles, and at the end
of the sad movie, the tears on my face

are not only my own. But now the outside
feels all wrong—trees not breathing,

sidewalks unspeckled by a single freckle,
and blazing over everything, a faceless sun.

JACK GILBERT
(1925–2012)

Failing and Flying

Everyone forgets that Icarus also flew.
It's the same when love comes to an end,
or the marriage fails and people say
they knew it was a mistake, that everybody
said it would never work. That she was
old enough to know better. But anything
worth doing is worth doing badly.
Like being there by that summer ocean
on the other side of the island while
love was fading out of her, the stars
burning so extravagantly those nights that
anyone could tell you they would never last.
Every morning she was asleep in my bed
like a visitation, the gentleness in her
like antelope standing in the dawn mist.
Each afternoon I watched her coming back
through the hot stony field after swimming,
the sea light behind her and the huge sky
on the other side of that. Listened to her
while we ate lunch. How can they say
the marriage failed? Like the people who
came back from Provence (when it was Provence)
and said it was pretty but the food was greasy.
I believe Icarus was not failing as he fell,
but just coming to the end of his triumph.

March

Crystal Declension

Well, two things are certain —
                                the sun will rise and the sun will set.
Most everything else is up for grabs.
It's back on its way down now
As a mother moose and her twin calves
Step lightly, lightly
                    across the creek through the understory
And half-lit grasses,
Then disappear in a clutch of willow bushes.
                                    If one, anyone,
Could walk through his own life as delicately, as sure,
As she did, all wreckage, all deadfall,
Would stay sunlight, and ring like crystal among the trees.

HAZEL HALL
(1886–1924)

Two Sewing

The wind is sewing with needles of rain.
With shining needles of rain
It stitches into the thin
Cloth of earth. In,
In, in, in.
Oh, the wind has often sewed with me.
One, two, three.

Spring must have fine things
To wear like other springs.
Of silken green the grass must be
Embroidered. *One and two and three.*
Then every crocus must be made
So subtly as to seem afraid
Of lifting colour from the ground;
And after crocuses the round
Heads of tulips, and all the fair
Intricate garb that Spring will wear.
The wind must sew with needles of rain,
With shining needles of rain,
Stitching into the thin
Cloth of earth, in,
In, in, in,
For all the springs of futurity.
One, two, three.

Alcove

Is it possible that spring could be
once more approaching? We forget each time
what a mindless business it is, porous like sleep,
adrift on the horizon, refusing to take sides, "mugwump
of the final hour," lest an agenda—horrors!—be imputed to it,
and the whole point of its being spring collapse
like a hole dug in sand. It's breathy, though,
you have to say that for it.

And should further seasons coagulate
into years, like spilled, dried paint, why,
who's to say we weren't provident? We indeed
looked out for others as though they mattered, and they,
catching the spirit, came home with us, spent the night
in an alcove from which their breathing could be heard clearly.
But it's not over yet. Terrible incidents happen
daily. That's how we get around obstacles.

SARAH GAMBITO
(1973–)

Yolanda: A Typhoon

How much our hands are God's

to be running fingers over braille cities.

We are this hand pushed through our womb.

Weeping with each other's blood in our eyes.

I dreamed that I slept with the light on.

I was asleep in my mother's bed because my father was out to sea

and my claim on him was to feel the frets of my death sure to come.

Sweet, small fishing rod. Ears of wind rushing through many jellied trees.

We were on this cardboard earth with its puffing volcanoes

miniature baseball players and horrible winds

scored by musician's hands.

Stand in the strong ear of this love.

Serenity

Brook,
Be still,—be still!
Midnight's arch is broken
In thy ceaseless ripples.
Dark and cold below them
Runs the troubled water,—
Only on its bosom,
Shimmering and trembling,
Doth the glinted star-shine
        Sparkle and cease.

Life,
Be still,—be still!
Boundless truth is shattered
On thy hurrying current.
Rest, with face uplifted,
Calm, serenely quiet;
Drink the deathless beauty—
Thrills of love and wonder
Sinking, shining, star-like;
Till the mirrored heaven
Hollow down within thee
Holy deeps unfathomed,
Where far thoughts go floating,
And low voices wander
        Whispering peace.

RALPH BURNS
(1949–)

Fishing in Winter

A man staring at a small lake sees
his father cast light line out over
the willows. He's forgotten his
father has been dead for two years
and the lake is where a blue fog
rolls, and the sky could be, if it
were black or blue or white,
the backdrop of all attention.

He wades out to join the father,
following where the good strikes
seem to lead. It's cold. The shape
breath takes on a cold day is like
anything else—a rise on a small lake,
the Oklahoma hills, blue scrub—
a shape already inside a shape,
two songs, two breaths on the water.

DANA GOODYEAR
(1976–)

Séance at Tennis

I play with an old boyfriend, to tease you out.
In white shorts that you've never seen before.
You storm — wind, panic in the tree.
Rattling like the genius
like the jealous man.
Making it impossible to hit.
So nothing clears the net.
An inside joke, my comingback love:
He can't return, but you can?

After an hour, the court is swept, and reassumes
the waiting face of the bereft. But *you* —
the sky turns blue with your held breath.

TRACI BRIMHALL
(1982–)

The Last Known Sighting
of the Mapinguari

Before she died, my mother told me
I'd make the monster that would kill me,
so I knew this was someone else's death
creeping into my field, butchering my cow.
I recognized its lone eye and two mouths.
Perhaps it mistook the lowing for the call
of its own kind. I didn't mind the heifer—
she'd been sick for weeks, her death a mercy—
but her calf circled, refusing to leave even
as the creature pulled out its mother's tongue,
fed one of its mouths and moaned from the other.
The intestines glowed dully in the moonlight.
The calf bawled. The disappointed mapinguari
sat, thousands of worms rising out of the split
heart it held, testing the strange night air.
I've outlived all the miracles that came for me.
My mother was wrong and not wrong,
like the calf who approached the monster
and licked the blood from its fingers.

Tackle Football

Snow up to our waists and coming down still.
There was a field here once, when we began.
We marked the end zones and set up the goals.

Now nobody can even move, much less tackle.
I am Ganymede fleeing on a temple frieze.
We stand around like lovesick Neanderthals.

We're Pompeian before Pompeii was hot.
We have the aspect of the classic dead
Or of stranded, shivering astronauts.

It was early in the era of the pause button:
We paused and paused the afternoons away
Indoors, blasting our ballistic erections

At the blurred bikinis of celebrities,
Then, splaying on the linoleum floor,
Awaited the apportioned pizza delivery.

Now, someone has paused us, or so it appears,
But they didn't pause the snow, or the hour:
As the one gets higher, the other gets later.

AARON SMITH
(1974–)

Like Him

I'm almost forty and just understanding my father
doesn't like me. At thirteen I quit basketball, the next year
refused to hunt, I knew he was disappointed, but never
thought he didn't have to like me
to love me. No girls. Never learned
to drive a stick. Chose the kitchen and mom
while he went to the woods with friends who had sons
like he wanted. He tried fishing—a rod and reel
under the tree one Christmas. Years I tried
talking deeper, acting tougher
when we were together. Last summer
I went with him to buy a tractor.
In case he needs help, Mom said. He didn't look at me
as he and the sales guy tied the wheels to the trailer, perfect
boy-scout knots. Why do I sometimes wish I could be a man
who cares about cars and football, who carries a pocketknife
and needs it? It was January when he screamed: *I'm not
a student, don't talk down to me!* I yelled: *You're not smart enough
to be one!* I learned to fight like his father, like him, like men:
the meanest guy wins, don't ever apologize.

LOLA RIDGE
(1873–1941)

Scandal

Aren't there bigger things to talk about
Than a window in Greenwich Village
And hyacinths sprouting
Like little puce poems out of a sick soul?
Some cosmic hearsay—
As to whom—it can't be Mars!
   put the moon—that way . . . .
Or what winds do to canyons
Under the tall stars . . .
Or even
How that old roué, Neptune,
Cranes over his bald-head moons
At the twinkling heel of a sky-scraper.

VIJAY SESHADRI
(1954–)

Survivor

We hold it against you that you survived.
People better than you are dead,
but you still punch the clock.
Your body has wizened but has not bled

its substance out on the killing floor
or flatlined in intensive care
or vanished after school
or stepped off the ledge in despair.

Of all those you started with,
only you are still around;
only you have not been listed with
the defeated and the drowned.

So how could you ever win our respect? —
you, who had the sense to duck,
you, with your strength almost intact
and all your good luck.

Borderline Mambo

As if the lid stayed put on the marmalade.
As if you could get the last sip of champagne
out of the bottom of the fluted glass.
As if we weren't all dying, as if we all weren't
going to die some time, as if we knew for certain
when, or how. As if the baseball scores made sense
to the toddler. As if the dance steps mattered, or there's a point
where they don't. For instance wheelchair. Heart flutter.
Oxygen bottle mounted on the septuagenarian's back
at the state ballroom competitions—that's Manny,
still pumping the mambo with his delicious slip
of an instructor, hip hip hooray. Mambo, for instance,
if done right, gives you a chance to rest: one beat in four.
One chance in four, one chance in ten, a hundred, as if
we could understand what that means. Hooray. Keep
pumping. As if you could keep the lid on a secret
once the symptoms start to make sense. A second
instance, a respite. A third. Always that hope.
If we could just scrape that last little bit
out, if only it wouldn't bottom out
before they can decode the message
sent to the cells. Of course it matters when, even though
(because?) we live in mystery. For instance
Beauty. Love. Honor. As if we didn't like
secrets. Point where it hurts. Of course we'll tell.

RAFAEL CAMPO
(1964–)

Hospital Writing Workshop

Arriving late, my clinic having run
past 6 again, I realize I don't
have cancer, don't have HIV, like them,
these students who are patients, who I lead
in writing exercises, reading poems.
For them, this isn't academic, it's
reality: I ask that they describe
an object right in front of them, to make
it come alive, and one writes about death,
her death, as if by just imagining
the softness of its skin, its panting rush
into her lap, that she might tame it; one
observes instead the love he lost, he's there,
beside him in his gown and wheelchair,
together finally again. I take
a good, long breath; we're quiet as newborns.
The little conference room grows warm, and right
before my eyes, I see that what I thought
unspeakable was more than this, was hope.

LAURA KASISCHKE
(1961–)

Near misses

The truck that swerved to miss the stroller in which I slept.

My mother turning from the laundry basket just in time to see me open
the third-story window to call to the cat.

In the car, on ice, something spinning and made of history snatched me
back from the guardrail and set me down between two gentle trees.
And that time I thought to look both ways on the one-way street.

And when the doorbell rang, and I didn't answer, and just before I slipped
one night into a drunken dream, I remembered to blow out the candle
burning on the table beside me.

It's a miracle, I tell you, this middle-aged woman scanning the cans on
the grocery store shelf. Hidden in the works of a mysterious clock are
her many deaths, and yet the whole world is piled up before her on a
banquet table again today. The timer, broken. The sunset smeared
across the horizon in the girlish cursive of the ocean, *Forever, For You*.

And still she can offer only her body as proof:

The way it moves a little slower every day. And the cells, ticking away.
A crow pecking at a sweater. The last hour waiting patiently on a tray
for her somewhere in the future. The spoon slipping quietly into the
beautiful soup.

WALT WHITMAN
(1819–1892)

Miracles

Why, who makes much of a miracle?
As to me I know of nothing else but miracles,
Whether I walk the streets of Manhattan,
Or dart my sight over the roofs of houses toward the sky,
Or wade with naked feet along the beach just in the edge of the water,
Or stand under trees in the woods,
Or talk by day with any one I love, or sleep in the bed at night with any
    one I love,
Or sit at table at dinner with the rest,
Or look at strangers opposite me riding in the car,
Or watch honey-bees busy around the hive of a summer forenoon,
Or animals feeding in the fields,
Or birds, or the wonderfulness of insects in the air,
Or the wonderfulness of the sundown, or of stars shining so quiet and bright,
Or the exquisite delicate thin curve of the new moon in spring;
These with the rest, one and all, are to me miracles,
The whole referring, yet each distinct and in its place.

To me every hour of the light and dark is a miracle,
Every cubic inch of space is a miracle,
Every square yard of the surface of the earth is spread with the same,
Every foot of the interior swarms with the same.

To me the sea is a continual miracle,
The fishes that swim—the rocks—the motion of the waves—the ships
    with men in them,
What stranger miracles are there?

first green flare

makes
the air

quiver
and dart

the throat
ache

to call
makes

the heart
cheer

the ear
keen

to the sheer
glorious

windfall
of oriole

veery
vireo

KURT BROWN
(1944–2013)

Fisherman

A man spends his whole life fishing in himself
for something grand. It's like some lost lunker, big enough
to break all records. But he's only heard rumors, myths,
vague promises of wonder. He's only felt the shadow
of something enormous darken his life. Or has he?
Maybe it's the shadow of other fish, greater than his,
the shadow of other men's souls passing over him.
Each day he grabs his gear and makes his way
to the ocean. At least he's sure of that: or is he? Is it the ocean
or the little puddle of his tears? Is this his dinghy
or the frayed boards of his ego, scoured by storm?
He shoves off, feeling the land fall away under his boots.
Soon he's drifting under clouds, wind whispering blandishments
in his ears. It could be today: the water heaves
and settles like a chest . . . He's not far out.
It's all so pleasant, so comforting—the sunlight,
the waves. He'll go back soon, thinking: "Maybe tonight."
Night with its concealments, its shadow masking all other shadows.
Night with its privacies, its alluringly distant stars.

NAOMI SHIHAB NYE
(1952–)

The Rider

A boy told me
if he roller-skated fast enough
his loneliness couldn't catch up to him,

the best reason I ever heard
for trying to be a champion.

What I wonder tonight
pedaling hard down King William Street
is if it translates to bicycles.

A victory! To leave your loneliness
panting behind you on some street corner
while you float free into a cloud of sudden azaleas,
pink petals that have never felt loneliness,
no matter how slowly they fell.

ADA LIMÓN
(1976–)

The Conditional

Say tomorrow doesn't come.
Say the moon becomes an icy pit.
Say the sweet-gum tree is petrified.
Say the sun's a foul black tire fire.
Say the owl's eyes are pinpricks.
Say the raccoon's a hot tar stain.
Say the shirt's plastic ditch-litter.
Say the kitchen's a cow's corpse.
Say we never get to see it: bright
future, stuck like a bum star, never
coming close, never dazzling.
Say we never meet her. Never him.
Say we spend our last moments staring
at each other, hands knotted together,
clutching the dog, watching the sky burn.
Say, It doesn't matter. Say, That would be
enough. Say you'd still want this: us alive,
right here, feeling lucky.

CAROL MUSKE-DUKES
(1945–)

After Skate

He glides in on his single wing, after the signs go up. After
the truck leaves with the bunkbeds, grill, broken hall mirror.
After Scout is dropped off at the shelter. After the last look,

on the dying lawn. In the backyard, where the empty pool
stands open; he pops an ollie over the cracked patterns of tile:
tidal waves in neat squares. He kneels, checking angle against

depth. He lifts off where the board once leapt and leapt: cannon-
balls, swans: endless summer. He hurtles downward, kickturning,
sparks grinding hard on gunnite. Round the bend: the kidney,

the heart. The stone path where once glowed tiki torches at
the kingdom's ukelele gate. He rockets out of the dead lots each
day, past swingsets and shut-off sprinklers, his board struck up

from whirlwind. Nobody's home to the ownerless: he turns
inside their names, never minds ghosts, nothing in his wake.

AMY LOWELL
(1874–1925)

Vernal Equinox

The scent of hyacinths, like a pale mist, lies between me and my book;
And the South Wind, washing through the room,
Makes the candles quiver.
My nerves sting at a spatter of rain on the shutter,
And I am uneasy with the thrusting of green shoots
Outside, in the night.

Why are you not here to overpower me with your
    tense and urgent love?

WILLIAM WORDSWORTH
(1770–1850)

Lines Written in Early Spring

I heard a thousand blended notes,
While in a grove I sate reclined,
In that sweet mood when pleasant thoughts
Bring sad thoughts to the mind.

To her fair works did Nature link
The human soul that through me ran;
And much it grieved my heart to think
What man has made of man.

Through primrose tufts, in that sweet bower,
The periwinkle trailed its wreaths;
And 'tis my faith that every flower
Enjoys the air it breathes.

The birds around me hopped and played;
Their thoughts I cannot measure:—
But the least motion which they made,
It seemed a thrill of pleasure.

The budding twigs spread out their fan,
To catch the breezy air;
And I must think, do all I can,
That there was pleasure there.

If this belief from Heaven is sent,
If such be Nature's holy plan,
Have I not reason to lament
What man has made of man?

Spring Snow

A spring snow coincides with plum blossoms.
In a month, you will forget, then remember
when nine ravens perched in the elm sway in wind.

I will remember when I brake to a stop,
and a hubcap rolls through the intersection.
An angry man grinds pepper onto his salad;

it is how you nail a tin amulet ear
into the lintel. If, in deep emotion, we are
possessed by the idea of possession,

we can never lose to recover what is ours.
Sounds of an abacus are amplified and condensed
to resemble sounds of hail on a tin roof,

but mind opens to the smell of lightning.
Bodies were vaporized to shadows by intense heat;
in memory people outline bodies on walls.

Sonnet on a Line from Vénus Khoury-Ghata

She recognized the seasons by their texture
like flannel sheets or thick-piled bath-sized towels
like white asparagus or colored vowels
whose scabby bark elicited conjecture.
She recognized the seasons by their light
as flowering plants and bushes, keyed to measure
its length, wake briefly or unroll at leisure
beneath it: even when it's cold, the night
holds off; the long and reminiscent dusk
is like a pardon or a friend returned
whom she thought elsewhere, subtracted forever,
eclipsed in distance. Though the plants can't bask
in heat, darkness delays, and they discern
what equilibrium they can recover.

SHERWOOD ANDERSON
(1876–1941)

Spring Song

In the forest, amid old trees and wet dead leaves, a shrine.
Men on the wet leaves kneeling.
The spirit of God in the air above a shrine.

Now, America, you press your lips to mine,
Feel on your lips the throbbing of my blood.
Christ, come to life and life calling,
Sweet and strong.

Spring. God in the air above old fields.
Farmers marking fields for the planting of the corn.
Fields marked for corn to stand in long straight aisles.

In the spring I press your body down on wet cold new-plowed ground.
Men, give your souls to me.
I would have my sacred way with you.

In the forest, amid old trees and wet dead leaves, a shrine.
Men rising from the kneeling place to sing.
Everywhere in the fields now the orderly planting of corn.

D. H. LAWRENCE
(1885–1930)

The Enkindled Spring

This spring as it comes bursts up in bonfires green,
Wild puffing of emerald trees, and flame-filled bushes,
Thorn-blossom lifting in wreaths of smoke between
Where the wood fumes up and the watery, flickering rushes.

I am amazed at this spring, this conflagration
Of green fires lit on the soil of the earth, this blaze
Of growing, and sparks that puff in wild gyration,
Faces of people streaming across my gaze.

And I, what fountain of fire am I among
This leaping combustion of spring? My spirit is tossed
About like a shadow buffeted in the throng
Of flames, a shadow that's gone astray, and is lost.

WILLIAM CARLOS WILLIAMS
(1883–1963)

Spring Storm

The sky has given over
its bitterness.
Out of the dark change
all day long
rain falls and falls
as if it would never end.
Still the snow keeps
its hold on the ground.
But water, water
from a thousand runnels!
It collects swiftly,
dappled with black
cuts a way for itself
through green ice in the gutters.
Drop after drop it falls
from the withered grass-stems
of the overhanging embankment.

ROBERT FROST
(1874–1963)

To the Thawing Wind

Come with rain, O loud Southwester!
Bring the singer, bring the nester;
Give the buried flower a dream;
Make the settled snowbank steam;
Find the brown beneath the white;
But whate'er you do tonight,
Bathe my window, make it flow,
Melt it as the ice will go;
Melt the glass and leave the sticks
Like a hermit's crucifix;
Burst into my narrow stall;
Swing the picture on the wall;
Run the rattling pages o'er;
Scatter poems on the floor;
Turn the poet out of door.

CARL PHILLIPS
(1959–)

If a Wilderness

Then spring came:
                    branches-in-a-wind . . .

I bought a harness, I bought a bridle.
I wagered on God in a kind stranger—
kind at first; strange, then less so—
and I was right.
                    The difference between
God and luck is that luck, when it leaves,
does not go far: the idea is to believe
you could almost touch it . . .

                              Now he's
singing, cadence of a rough sea—A way of
crossing a dark so unspecific, it seems
everywhere: isn't that what singing, once,
was for?
          I lay the harness across my lap,
the bridle beside me for the sweat—the color
and smell of it—that I couldn't, by now,
lift the leather free of, even if I wanted to.

I don't want to.

JERICHO BROWN
(1976–)

Another Elegy

To believe in God is to love
What none can see. Let a lover go,

Let him walk out with the good
Spoons or die

Without a signature, and so much
Remains for scrubbing, for a polish

Cleaner than devotion. Tonight,
God is one spot, and you,

You must be one blind nun. You
Wipe, you rub, but love won't move.

April

MONICA FERRELL
(1975–)

Poetry

There is nothing beautiful here
However I may want it. I can't
Spin a crystal palace of this thin air,
Weave a darkness plush as molefur with my tongue
However I want. Yet I am not alone
In these alleys of vowels, which comfort me
As the single living nun of a convent
Is comforted by the walls of that catacomb
She walks at night, lit by her own moving candle.
I am not afraid of mirrors or the future
—Or even *you*, lovers, wandering cow-fat
And rutting in the gardens of this earthly verge
Where I too trod, a sunspot, parasol-shaded,
Kin to the trees, the bees, the color green.

E. E. CUMMINGS
(1894–1962)

somewhere I have never travelled,gladly beyond (LVII)

somewhere i have never travelled,gladly beyond
any experience,your eyes have their silence:
in your most frail gesture are things which enclose me,
or which i cannot touch because they are too near

your slightest look easily will unclose me
though i have closed myself as fingers,
you open always petal by petal myself as Spring opens
(touching skilfully,mysteriously)her first rose

or if your wish be to close me,i and
my life will shut very beautifully,suddenly,
as when the heart of this flower imagines
the snow carefully everywhere descending;

nothing which we are to perceive in this world equals
the power of your intense fragility:whose texture
compels me with the colour of its countries,
rendering death and forever with each breathing

(i do not know what it is about you that closes
and opens;only something in me understands
the voice of your eyes is deeper than all roses)
nobody,not even the rain,has such small hands

SARA TEASDALE
(1884–1933)

I Love You

When April bends above me
   And finds me fast asleep,
Dust need not keep the secret
   A live heart died to keep.

When April tells the thrushes,
   The meadow-larks will know,
And pipe the three words lightly
   To all the winds that blow.

Above his roof the swallows,
   In notes like far-blown rain,
Will tell the chirping sparrow
   Beside his window-pane.

O sparrow, little sparrow,
   When I am fast asleep,
Then tell my love the secret
   That I have died to keep.

The Gift

In memory of Ruth Stone
(June 8th, 1915–November 19th, 2011)

"All I did was write them down
wherever I was at the time, hanging
laundry, baking bread, driving to Illinois.
My name was attached to them
on the page but not in my head
because the bird I listened to outside
my window said I couldn't complain
about the blank in place of my name
if I wished to hold both ends of the wire
like a wire and continue to sing instead
of complain. It was my plight, my thorn,
my gift—the one word in three I was
permitted to call it by the Muse who took
mercy on me as long as I didn't explain."

HOA NGUYEN
(1967–)

Swell

Swell   you can dream more   the earth
swells   seeds pop
I glance at the prize
eyes closed in the glancing

It's not a time to run
I wear soft shoes
and it took a long time
to walk here

Insects nudge me in my dreams
like the 5 honey bees plus
the strange one
Intelligent bee glances buzzing

to say   Let me out   The fake
lights confuse us
confuses the source

Worker bee buzzed my neck
directly   me not turning off
lamps fast enough

Please
        just open the door
to the sun

WILLIAM CULLEN BRYANT
(1794–1878)

The Gladness of Nature

Is this a time to be cloudy and sad,
   When our mother Nature laughs around;
When even the deep blue heavens look glad,
   And gladness breathes from the blossoming ground

There are notes of joy from the hang-bird and wren,
   And the gossip of swallows through all the sky;
The ground-squirrel gayly chirps by his den,
   And the wilding bee hums merrily by.

The clouds are at play in the azure space
   And their shadows at play on the bright-green vale,
And here they stretch to the frolic chase,
   And there they roll on the easy gale.

There's a dance of leaves in that aspen bower,
   There's a titter of winds in that beechen tree,
There's a smile on the fruit, and a smile on the flower,
   And a laugh from the brook that runs to the sea.

And look at the broad-faced sun, how he smiles
   On the dewy earth that smiles in his ray,
On the leaping waters and gay young isles;
   Ay, look, and he'll smile thy gloom away.

THOMAS MEYER
(1947–)

Are You Going to Stay?

What was it I was going to say?
Slipped away probably because
it needn't be said. At that edge

almost not knowing but second
guessing the gain, loss, or effect
of an otherwise hesitant remark.

Slant of light on a brass box. The way
a passing thought knots the heart.
There's nothing, nothing to say.

CLAUDE MCKAY
(1889–1948)

Spring in New Hampshire

(To J.L.J.F.E.)

Too green the springing April grass,
    Too blue the silver-speckled sky,
For me to linger here, alas,
    While happy winds go laughing by,
Wasting the golden hours indoors,
Washing windows and scrubbing floors.

Too wonderful the April night,
    Too faintly sweet the first May flowers,
The stars too gloriously bright,
    For me to spend the evening hours,
When fields are fresh and streams are leaping,
Wearied, exhausted, dully sleeping.

Rain

Bobby flew out from his body
    on Nine Mile Hill.
You could say it was a Navajo semi
    careening down the earth
or his wife, pregnant and drunk
    who caused his lick of death

But what captured him was a light in the river
    folding open and open
blood, heart and stones
    shimmering like the Milky Way.

And then it rained.
What went down sucked the current,
took hold.

Now southern California falls into the ocean.
Now Phoenix struggles under water.

Something has been let loose in rain;
it is teaching us to love.

REGINALD GIBBONS
(1947–)

After Mandelshtam

To the futile sound
of midnight church bells,
out back someone is
rinsing her thoughts in
unfathomable
universal sky—
a cold faint glowing.
As always stars glint
white as salt on the
blade of an old axe.
Like mica in soil.
The rain-barrel's full,
there's ice in its mouth.
Smash the ice—comets
and stars melt away
like salt, the water
darkens and the earth
on which the barrel
stands is transparent
underfoot, and there
too are galaxies,
ghost-pale, silent in
the seven-thousand-
odd chambers of our
inhuman being.

GERTRUDE STEIN
(1874–1946)

Tender Buttons
[A light in the moon]

A light in the moon the only light is on Sunday. What was the sensible decision. The sensible decision was that notwithstanding many declarations and more music, not even notwithstanding the choice and a torch and a collection, notwithstanding the celebrating hat and a vacation and even more noise than cutting, notwithstanding Europe and Asia and being overbearing, not even notwithstanding an elephant and a strict occasion, not even withstanding more cultivation and some seasoning, not even with drowning and with the ocean being encircling, not even with more likeness and any cloud, not even with terrific sacrifice of pedestrianism and a special resolution, not even more likely to be pleasing. The care with which the rain is wrong and the green is wrong and the white is wrong, the care with which there is a chair and plenty of breathing. The care with which there is incredible justice and likeness, all this makes a magnificent asparagus, and also a fountain.

LUCILLE CLIFTON
(1936–2010)

the earth is a living thing

is a black shambling bear
ruffling its wild back and tossing
mountains into the sea

is a black hawk circling
the burying ground circling the bones
picked clean and discarded

is a fish black blind in the belly of water
is a diamond blind in the black belly of coal

is a black and living thing
is a favorite child
of the universe
feel her rolling her hand
in its kinky hair
feel her brushing it clean

JENNIFER CHANG
(1976–)

Pastoral

Something in the field is
working away. Root-noise.
Twig-noise. Plant
of weak chlorophyll, no
name for it. Something
in the field has mastered
distance by living too close
to fences. Yellow fruit, has it
pit or seeds? Stalk of wither. Grass-
noise fighting weed-noise. Dirt
and chant. Something in the
field. Coreopsis. I did not mean
to say that. Yellow petal, has it
wither-gift? Has it gorgeous
rash? Leaf-loss and worried
sprout, its bursting art. Some-
thing in the. Field fallowed and
cicada. I did not mean to
say. Has it roar and bloom?
Has it road and follow? A thistle
prick, fraught burrs, such
easy attachment. Stem-
and stamen-noise. Can I lime-
flower? Can I chamomile?
Something in the field cannot.

SUSAN HOWE
(1937–)

from Debths

A work of art is a world of signs, at least to the poet's nursery
bookshelf sheltered behind the artist's ear. I recall each little
motto howling its ins and outs to those of us who might as
well be on the moon illu illu illu

—

Antique Mirror
Etce ce Tera. Forgotn quiet all. Nobody grows old and crafty
here in middle air together. Long ago ice wraith foliage.
I had such fren

—

Our mother of puddled images fading away into deep blue polymer.
Seaweed, nets, shells, fish, feathers

TROY JOLLIMORE
(1971–)

On the Origins of Things

Everyone knows that the moon started out
as a renegade fragment of the sun, a solar
flare that fled that hellish furnace
and congealed into a flat frozen pond suspended
between the planets. But did you know
that anger began as music, played
too often and too loudly by drunken performers
at weddings and garden parties? Or that turtles
evolved from knuckles, ice from tears, and darkness
from misunderstanding? As for the dominant
thesis regarding the origin of love, I
abstain from comment, nor will I allow
myself to address the idea that dance
began as a kiss, that happiness was
an accidental import from Spain, that the ancient
game of jump-the-fire gave rise
to politics. But I will confess
that I began as an astronomer—a liking
for bright flashes, vast distances, unreachable things,
a hand stretched always toward the furthest limit—
and that my longing for you has not taken me
very far from that original desire
to inscribe a comet's orbit around the walls
of our city, to gently stroke the surface of the stars.

EDGAR LEE MASTERS
(1868–1950)

Fiddler Jones

The earth keeps some vibration going
There in your heart, and that is you.
And if the people find you can fiddle,
Why, fiddle you must, for all your life.
What do you see, a harvest of clover?
Or a meadow to walk through to the river?
The wind's in the corn; you rub your hands
For beeves hereafter ready for market;
Or else you hear the rustle of skirts
Like the girls when dancing at Little Grove.
To Cooney Potter a pillar of dust
Or whirling leaves meant ruinous drouth;
They looked to me like Red-Head Sammy
Stepping it off, to "Toor-a-Loor."
How could I till my forty acres
Not to speak of getting more,
With a medley of horns, bassoons and piccolos
Stirred in my brain by crows and robins
And the creak of a wind-mill—only these?
And I never started to plow in my life
That some one did not stop in the road
And take me away to a dance or picnic.
I ended up with forty acres;
I ended up with a broken fiddle—
And a broken laugh, and a thousand memories,
And not a single regret.

JANE HIRSHFIELD
(1953–)

The Supple Deer

The quiet opening
between fence strands
perhaps eighteen inches.

Antlers to hind hooves,
four feet off the ground,
the deer poured through.

No tuft of the coarse white belly hair left behind.

I don't know how a stag turns
into a stream, an arc of water.
I have never felt such accurate envy.

Not of the deer:

To be that porous, to have such largeness pass through me.

ADAM KIRSCH
(1976–)

Now that no one looking at the night–

Now that no one looking at the night–
Sky blanked by leakage from electric lamps
And headlights prowling through the parking lot
Could recognize the Babylonian dance
That once held every gazer; now that spoons
And scales, and swordsmen battling with beasts
Have decomposed into a few stars strewn
Illegibly across an empty space,
Maybe the old unfalsifiable
Predictions and extrapolated spheres
No longer need to be an obstacle
To hearing what it is the stars declare:
That there are things created of a size
We can't and weren't meant to understand,
As fish know nothing of the sun that writes
Its bright glyphs on the black waves overhead.

WILLA CATHER
(1873–1947)

Prairie Spring

Evening and the flat land,
Rich and sombre and always silent;
The miles of fresh-plowed soil,
Heavy and black, full of strength and harshness;
The growing wheat, the growing weeds,
The toiling horses, the tired men;
The long empty roads,
Sullen fires of sunset, fading,
The eternal, unresponsive sky.
Against all this, Youth,
Flaming like the wild roses,
Singing like the larks over the plowed fields,
Flashing like a star out of the twilight;
Youth with its insupportable sweetness,
Its fierce necessity,
Its sharp desire,
Singing and singing,
Out of the lips of silence,
Out of the earthy dusk.

JOANNA KLINK
(1969–)

from 3 Bewildered Landscapes

STARS, SCATTERSTILL. Constellations of people and quiet.

Those nights when nothing catches, nothing also is artless.

I walked for hours in those forests, my legs a canvas of scratches,

trading on the old hopes—*we were meant to be lost.* But being lost

means not knowing what it means. Inside the meadow is the grass,

rich with darkness. Inside the grass is the wish to be rooted, inside the rain

the wish to dissolve. What you think you live for you may not live for.

One star goes out. One breath lifts inside a crow inside a field.

VIJAY SESHADRI
(1954–)

Heaven

There's drought on the mountain.
Wildfires scour the hills.
So the mammal crawls down the desiccated rills
searching for the fountain,

which it finds, believe it or not,
or sort of finds. A thin silver sliver
rises from an underground river
and makes a few of the hot

rocks steam and the pebbles hiss.
Soon the mammal will drink,
but it has first
to stop and think
its reflexive, impeccable thought:
that thinking comes down to this—
mystery, longing, thirst.

HEATHER CHRISTLE
(1980–)

Such and Such a Time at Such and Such a Palace

The lack of a single-word infinitive
in our language is what is killing me

this morning
                          A single word for all
infinitives is what God is doing tonight

This is just one of many acts
to have passed through the garden

Previously on this show they put
a peacock back together wrong

after its demise
                          Something
there was in the syntax

Poor bird could feel it in his bones

ANNE WALDMAN
(1945–)

The V of them

the V of them   wind
  a chevron   claw
   zigzag   bird
    against wind   a
     meander   column
      bilateral   comb
       forked tail   axe
        lozenge   V
         circles   then
          in   hoop
           egg or   spiral
            checker   pattern
                  board
                shape

Never

The clouds' disintegrating script
spells out the word *squander.*

Tree shadows lie down in the field.
Clipped to a grass blade's underside,

a crisp green grasshopper
weighs down the tip,

swaying between birth and death.
I'll think of him as we clink

glasses with the guests,
eating olives as the sun goes down.

ROBERT PENN WARREN
(1905–1989)

Vision

I shall build me a house where the larkspur blooms
    In a narrow glade in an alder wood,
Where the sunset shadows make violet glooms,
    And a whip-poor-will calls in eerie mood.

I shall lie on a bed of river sedge,
    And listen to the glassy dark,
With a guttered light on my window ledge,
    While an owl stares in at me white and stark.

I shall burn my house with the rising dawn,
    And leave but the ashes and smoke behind,
And again give the glade to the owl and the fawn,
    When the grey wood smoke drifts away with the wind.

JEAN TOOMER
(1894–1967)

Storm Ending

Thunder blossoms gorgeously above our heads,
Great, hollow, bell-like flowers,
Rumbling in the wind,
Stretching clappers to strike our ears . . .
Full-lipped flowers
Bitten by the sun
Bleeding rain
Dripping rain like golden honey—
And the sweet earth flying from the thunder.

JOSEPH MILLAR
(1945–)

One Day

Everything shimmers
with the sound of the train
rattling over the bridge
especially the ears and nostrils and teeth
of the horse riding out
to the pasture of death
where the long train runs
on diesel fuel
that used to run on coal.
I keep listening
for the crickets and birds
and my words fall down below.

I mistook the train for a thunder storm,
I mistook the willow tree
for a home, it's nothing to brag about
when you think of it
spending this time all alone.
I wandered into the hay field
and two ticks jumped in my hair
they dug in my scalp
and drank up my blood
like the sweet wine of Virginia,
then left me under the Druid moon
down here on earth in the kingdom.

CHRISTINA ROSSETTI
(1830–1894)

Who Has Seen the Wind?

Who has seen the wind?
  Neither I nor you:
But when the leaves hang trembling
  The wind is passing thro'.

Who has seen the wind?
  Neither you nor I:
But when the trees bow down their heads
  The wind is passing by.

Thank You

If you find yourself half naked
and barefoot in the frosty grass, hearing,
again, the earth's great, sonorous moan that says
you are the air of the now and gone, that says
all you love will turn to dust,
and will meet you there, do not
raise your fist. Do not raise
your small voice against it. And do not
take cover. Instead, curl your toes
into the grass, watch the cloud
ascending from your lips. Walk
through the garden's dormant splendor.
Say only, thank you.
Thank you.

BRIGIT PEGEEN KELLY
(1951–)

The Satyr's Heart

Now I rest my head on the satyr's carved chest,
The hollow where the heart would have been, if sandstone
Had a heart, if a headless goat man could have a heart.
His neck rises to a dull point, points upward
To something long gone, elusive, and at his feet
The small flowers swarm, earnest and sweet, a clamor
Of white, a clamor of blue, and black the sweating soil
They breed in . . . . If I sit without moving, how quickly
Things change, birds turning tricks in the trees,
Colorless birds and those with color, the wind fingering
The twigs, and the furred creatures doing whatever
Furred creatures do. So, and so. There is the smell of fruit
And the smell of wet coins. There is the sound of a bird
Crying, and the sound of water that does not move . . . .
If I pick the dead iris? If I wave it above me
Like a flag, a blazoned flag? My fanfare? Little fare
With which I buy my way, making things brave?
No, that is not it. Uncovering what is brave.
The way now I bend over and with my foot turn up a stone,
And there they are: the armies of pale creatures who
Without cease or doubt sew the sweet sad earth.

May

C. K. WILLIAMS
(1936–)

They Call This

A young mother on a motor scooter stopped at a traffic light, her little
son perched on the ledge between her legs; she in a gleaming helmet, he
in a replica of it, smaller, but the same color and just as shiny. His visor is
swung shut, hers is open.

As I pull up beside them on my bike, the mother is leaning over to
embrace the child, whispering something in his ear, and I'm shaken, truly
shaken, by the wish, the need, to have those slim strong arms contain me
in their sanctuary of affection.

Though they call this regression, though that implies a going back
to some other state and this has never left me, this fundamental pang
of being too soon torn from a bliss that promises more bliss, no matter
that the scooter's fenders are dented, nor that as it idles it pops, clears its
throat, growls.

CHRISTINA ROSSETTI
(1830–1894)

Sonnets are full of love, and this my tome

Sonnets are full of love, and this my tome
    Has many sonnets: so here now shall be
    One sonnet more, a love sonnet, from me
To her whose heart is my heart's quiet home,
    To my first Love, my Mother, on whose knee
I learnt love-lore that is not troublesome;
    Whose service is my special dignity,
And she my loadstar while I go and come.
And so because you love me, and because
    I love you, Mother, I have woven a wreath
        Of rhymes wherewith to crown your honoured name:
        In you not fourscore years can dim the flame
Of love, whose blessed glow transcends the laws
    Of time and change and mortal life and death.

EDGAR ALLAN POE
(1809–1849)

To My Mother

Because I feel that, in the Heavens above,
   The angels, whispering to one another,
Can find, among their burning terms of love,
   None so devotional as that of "Mother,"
Therefore by that dear name I long have called you—
   You who are more than mother unto me,
And fill my heart of hearts, where Death installed you
   In setting my Virginia's spirit free.
My mother—my own mother, who died early,
   Was but the mother of myself; but you
Are mother to the one I loved so dearly,
   And thus are dearer than the mother I knew
By that infinity with which my wife
   Was dearer to my soul than its soul-life.

LOLA RIDGE
(1873–1941)

Mother

Your love was like moonlight
turning harsh things to beauty,
so that little wry souls
reflecting each other obliquely
as in cracked mirrors . . .
beheld in your luminous spirit
their own reflection,
transfigured as in a shining stream,
and loved you for what they are not.

You are less an image in my mind
than a luster
I see you in gleams
pale as star-light on a gray wall . . .
evanescent as the reflection of a white swan
shimmering in broken water.

CATHERINE BARNETT
(1960–)

Chorus

So who mothers the mothers
who tend the hallways of mothers,
the spill of mothers, the smell of mothers,
who mend the eyes of mothers,
the lies of mothers scared
to turn on lights in basements
filled with mothers called by mothers in the dark,
the kin of mothers, the gin of mothers,
mothers out on bail,
who mothers the hail-mary mothers
asleep in their stockings
while the crows sing heigh ho carrion crow,
fol de riddle, lol de riddle,
carry on, carry on—

JAMES WELDON JOHNSON
(1871–1928)

Mother Night

Eternities before the first-born day,
    Or ere the first sun fledged his wings of flame,
    Calm Night, the everlasting and the same,
    A brooding mother over chaos lay.
And whirling suns shall blaze and then decay,
    Shall run their fiery courses and then claim
    The haven of the darkness whence they came;
    Back to Nirvanic peace shall grope their way.

So when my feeble sun of life burns out,
    And sounded is the hour for my long sleep,
    I shall, full weary of the feverish light,
Welcome the darkness without fear or doubt,
    And heavy-lidded, I shall softly creep
    Into the quiet bosom of the Night.

ARCHIBALD MACLEISH
(1892–1982)

An Eternity

There is no dusk to be,
  There is no dawn that was,
Only there's now, and now,
  And the wind in the grass.

Days I remember of
  Now in my heart, are now;
Days that I dream will bloom
  White peach bough.

Dying shall never be
  Now in the windy grass;
Now under shooken leaves
  Death never was.

DAVID YOUNG
(1936–)

Mother's Day

—for my children

I see her doing something simple, paying bills,
or leafing through a magazine or book,
and wish that I could say, and she could hear,

that now I start to understand her love
for all of us, the fullness of it.

It burns there in the past, beyond my reach,
a modest lamp.

The Violet

Down in a green and shady bed,
   A modest violet grew,
Its stalk was bent, it hung its head,
   As if to hide from view.

And yet it was a lovely flow'r,
   Its colours bright and fair;
It might have grac'd a rosy bow'r
   Instead of hiding there.

Yet there it was content to bloom,
   In modest tints array'd;
And there diffus'd its sweet perfume,
   Within the silent shade.

Then let me to the valley go,
   This pretty flow'r to see;
That I may also learn to grow
   In sweet humility.

WILLIAM BLAKE
(1757–1827)

Ah! Sun-flower

Ah Sun-flower! weary of time.
Who countest the steps of the Sun:
Seeking after that sweet golden clime.
Where the travellers journey is done.

Where the Youth pined away with desire.
And the pale Virgin shrouded in snow:
Arise from their graves and aspire.
Where my Sun-flower wishes to go.

PHILIP FRENEAU
(1752–1832)

The Wild Honey Suckle

Fair flower, that dost so comely grow,
Hid in this silent, dull retreat,
Untouched thy honied blossoms blow,
Unseen thy little branches greet:
    No roving foot shall crush thee here,
    No busy hand provoke a tear.

By Nature's self in white arrayed,
She bade thee shun the vulgar eye,
And planted here the guardian shade,
And sent soft waters murmuring by;
    Thus quietly thy summer goes,
    Thy days declining to repose.

Smit with those charms, that must decay,
I grieve to see your future doom;
They died—nor were those flowers more gay,
The flowers that did in Eden bloom;
    Unpitying frosts, and Autumn's power
    Shall leave no vestige of this flower.

From morning suns and evening dews
At first thy little being came:
If nothing once, you nothing lose,
For when you die you are the same;
    The space between, is but an hour,
    The frail duration of a flower.

LOUISE GLÜCK
(1943–)

The Red Poppy

The great thing
is not having
a mind. Feelings:
oh, I have those; they
govern me. I have
a lord in heaven
called the sun, and open
for him, showing him
the fire of my own heart, fire
like his presence.
What could such glory be
if not a heart? Oh my brothers and sisters,
were you like me once, long ago,
before you were human? Did you
permit yourselves
to open once, who would never
open again? Because in truth
I am speaking now
the way you do. I speak
because I am shattered.

VACHEL LINDSAY
(1879–1931)

The Dandelion

O dandelion, rich and haughty,
King of village flowers!
Each day is coronation time,
You have no humble hours.
I like to see you bring a troop
To beat the blue-grass spears,
To scorn the lawn-mower that would be
Like fate's triumphant shears.
Your yellow heads are cut away,
It seems your reign is o'er.
By noon you raise a sea of stars
More golden than before.

WILLIAM WORDSWORTH
(1770–1850)

The Daffodils

I wandered lonely as a cloud
   That floats on high o'er vales and hills,
When all at once I saw a crowd,
   A host, of golden daffodils;
Beside the lake, beneath the trees,
Fluttering and dancing in the breeze.

Continuous as the stars that shine
   And twinkle on the Milky Way,
They stretched in never-ending line
   Along the margin of a bay:
Ten thousand saw I at a glance,
Tossing their heads in sprightly dance.

The waves beside them danced, but they
   Out-did the sparkling waves in glee:
A Poet could not but be gay,
   In such a jocund company:
I gazed—and gazed—but little thought
What wealth the show to me had brought:

For oft, when on my couch I lie
   In vacant or in pensive mood,
They flash upon that inward eye
   Which is the bliss of solitude;
And then my heart with pleasure fills,
And dances with the daffodils.

ROBERT BURNS
(1759–1796)

O were my love
yon Lilac fair

O were my love yon Lilac fair,
  Wi' purple blossoms to the spring;
And I, a bird to shelter there,
  When wearied on my little wing;

How I wad mourn when it was torn
  By autumn wild, and winter rude!
But I wad sing on wanton wing,
  When youthfu' May its bloom renew'd.

O gin my love were yon red rose,
  That grows upon the castle wa',
And I mysel' a drap o' dew,
  Into her bonie breast to fa'!

O there, beyond expression blest,
  I'd feast on beauty a' the night;
Seal'd on her silk-saft faulds to rest,
  Till fley'd awa' by Phoebus' light!

ADRIENNE RICH
(1929–2012)

Tonight No Poetry Will Serve

Saw you walking barefoot
taking a long look
at the new moon's eyelid

later spread
sleep-fallen, naked in your dark hair
asleep but not oblivious
of the unslept unsleeping
elsewhere

Tonight I think
no poetry
will serve

Syntax of rendition:

verb pilots the plane
adverb modifies action

verb force-feeds noun
submerges the subject
noun is choking
verb   disgraced   goes on doing

now diagram the sentence

2007

In the Garden (M.H.)

We waited for the sun
To break its cloudy prison
(For day was not yet done,
And night still unbegun)
Leaning by the dial.

After many a trial—
We all silent there—
It burst as new-arisen,
Throwing a shade to where
Time travelled at that minute.

Little saw we in it,
But this much I know,
Of lookers on that shade,
Her towards whom it made
Soonest had to go.

JENNIFER BARTLETT
(1941–)

The sun rears

The sun rears her unlikely head
In this late spring,
I walk past rubber black boots decorated
With brightly colored umbrellas
In a useless attempt to block the rain.

Up the subway to 14th street
Around the corner to 12th
I climb to the tenth or the eighth floor
Depending on your bodily condition.

I keep vigil over this resting.
My body is a candle, glowing
Until you make the transition
Back into or out of this life.

This is among the things that could happen.
This is among the things that happened.
For now, you reside in imposed silence.
Dying is just another commodity and

The soul wants routine.
The soul wants sameness, boredom.
The soul wants *letting go.*

Over us, the palmed stars.

JAMES RUSSELL LOWELL
(1819–1891)

from Under the Willows

May is a pious fraud of the almanac,
A ghastly parody of real Spring
Shaped out of snow and breathed with eastern wind;
Or if, o'er-confident, she trust the date,
And, with her handful of anemones,
Herself as shivery, steal into the sun,
The season need but turn his hourglass round,
And Winter suddenly, like crazy Lear,
Reels back, and brings the dead May in his arms,
Her budding breasts and wan dislustred front
With frosty streaks and drifts of his white beard
All overblown. Then, warmly walled with books,
While my wood-fire supplies the sun's defect,
Whispering old forest-sagas in its dreams,
I take my May down from the happy shelf
Where perch the world's rare song-birds in a row,
Waiting my choice to open with full breast,
And beg an alms of spring-time, ne'er denied
Indoors by vernal Chaucer, whose fresh woods
Throb thick with merle and mavis all the year.

GWENDOLYN B. BENNETT
(1902–1981)

Sonnet—2

Some things are very dear to me—
Such things as flowers bathed by rain
Or patterns traced upon the sea
Or crocuses where snow has lain . . .
The iridescence of a gem,
The moon's cool opalescent light,
Azaleas and the scent of them,
And honeysuckles in the night.
And many sounds are also dear—
Like winds that sing among the trees
Or crickets calling from the weir

Or Negroes humming melodies.
But dearer far than all surmise
Are sudden tear-drops in your eyes.

102 Today

If Wystan Auden were alive today
he'd be a small tangle of black lines
on a rumpled white bedsheet,
his little eyes looking up at you.
What did you bring?
Some yellow daffodils and green stems.
Or did they bring you?

Auden once said,
"Where the hell is Bobby?"
and we looked around,
but there was no Bobby there.
Ah, Auden, no Bobby for you.
Just these daffodils in a clean white vase.

CORNELIUS EADY
(1954–)

The Gardenia

The trouble is, you can never take
That flower from Billie's hair.
She is always walking too fast
and try as we might,

there's no talking her into slowing.
Don't go down into that basement,
we'd like to scream. What will it take
to bargain her blues,

To retire that term when it comes
to her? But the grain and the cigarettes,
the narcs and the fancy-dressed boys,
the sediment in her throat.

That's the soil those petals spring from,
Like a fist, if a fist could sing.

H. D.
(1886–1961)

Sea Rose

Rose, harsh rose,
marred and with stint of petals,
meagre flower, thin,
sparse of leaf,

more precious
than a wet rose
single on a stem—
you are caught in the drift.

Stunted, with small leaf,
you are flung on the sand,
you are lifted
in the crisp sand
that drives in the wind.

Can the spice-rose
drip such acrid fragrance
hardened in a leaf?

ELLEN BRYANT VOIGT
(1943–)

Practice

To weep unbidden, to wake
at night in order to weep, to wait
for the whisker on the face of the clock
to twitch again, moving
the dumb day forward —

is this merely practice?
Some believe in heaven,
some in rest. *We'll float,*
you said. *Afterward*
we'll float between two worlds —

five bronze beetles
stacked like spoons in one
peony blossom, drugged by lust:
if I came back as a bird
I'd remember that —

until everyone we love
is safe is what you said.

LEE ANN BROWN
(1963–)

What is the Grass?

The child asks, bringing it to me in handfuls.
We stop at the Walt Whitman Service Area—
No sign of Him save some "Democratic Vistas"
& "Drum Taps" on a plaque near the Micky D's

Let's go find the grass
I say to my two-year-old beauty and
We pick one blade from the median
Then back we go in the forever car

Hours later, pulling into Richmond
She, half awake in my arms mumbles

Let's go find the grass

MADELON SPRENGNETHER
(1942–)

from The Angel of Duluth

I lied a little. There are things I don't want to tell you. How lonely I am today and sick at heart. How the rain falls steadily and cold on a garden grown greener, more lush and even less tame. I haven't done much, I confess, to contain it. The grapevine, as usual, threatens everything in its path, while the raspberry canes, aggressive and abundant, are clearly out of control. I'm afraid the wildflowers have taken over, being after all the most hardy and tolerant of shade and neglect. This year the violets and lilies of the valley are rampant, while the phlox are about to emit their shocking pink perfume. Oh, my dear, had you been here this spring, you would have seen how the bleeding hearts are thriving.

HARRYETTE MULLEN
(1953–)

from Tanka Diary

The botanical garden is just as I remember,
although it is certain that everything
has changed since my last visit.

How many hilarious questions these fuzzy
fiddleheads are inquiring of spring
will be answered as green ferns unfurl?

Walking the path, I stop to pick up
bleached bark from a tree, curled into
a scroll of ancient wisdom I am unable to read.

Even in my dreams I'm hiking
these mountain trails expecting to find a rock
that nature has shaped to remind me of a heart.

PHILLIS LEVIN
(1954–)

May Day

I've decided to waste my life again,
Like I used to: get drunk on
The light in the leaves, find a wall
Against which something can happen,

Whatever may have happened
Long ago—let a bullet hole echoing
The will of an executioner, a crevice
In which a love note was hidden,

Be a cell where a struggling tendril
Utters a few spare syllables at dawn.
I've decided to waste my life
In a new way, to forget whoever

Touched a hair on my head, because
It doesn't matter what came to pass,
Only that it passed, because we repeat
Ourselves, we repeat ourselves.

I've decided to walk a long way
Out of the way, to allow something
Dreaded to waken for no good reason,
Let it go without saying,

Let it go as it will to the place
It will go without saying: a wall
Against which a body was pressed
For no good reason, other than this.

Herb Garden

"And these, small, unobserved . . ." —Janet Lewis

The lizard, an exemplar of the small,
Spreads fine, adhesive digits to perform
Vertical push-ups on a sunny wall;
Bees grapple spikes of lavender, or swarm
The dill's gold umbels or low clumps of thyme.
Bored with its trellis, a resourceful rose
Has found a nearby cedar tree to climb
And to festoon with floral furbelows.

Though the great, heat-stunned sunflower looks half dead
The way it, shepherd's crook-like, hangs its head,
The herbs maintain their modest self-command:
Their fragrances and colors warmly mix
While, quarrying between the pathway's bricks,
Ants build minute volcanoes out of sand.

Leviathan

Truth also is the pursuit of it:
Like happiness, and it will not stand.

Even the verse begins to eat away
In the acid. Pursuit, pursuit;

A wind moves a little,
Moving in a circle, very cold.

How shall we say?
In ordinary discourse —

We must talk now. I am no longer sure of the words,
The clockwork of the world. What is inexplicable

Is the 'preponderance of objects,' The sky lights
Daily with that predominance

And we have become the present.

We must talk now. Fear
Is fear. But we abandon one another.

EMILY DICKINSON
(1830–1886)

Come Slowly—Eden! (211)

Come slowly—Eden!
Lips unused to Thee—
Bashful—sip thy Jessamines—
As the fainting Bee—

Reaching late his flower,
Round her chamber hums—
Counts his nectars—
Enters—and is lost in Balms.

June

MATTHEW ZAPRUDER
(1967–)

My Childhood

the orange ball arcs perfectly into the orange hoop

making a sound like a drawer closing

you will never get to hold that

I am here and nothing terrible will ever happen

across the street the giant white house full of kids

turns the pages of an endless book

the mother comes home and finds the child animal sleeping

I left my notebook beside the bed

the father came home and sat and quietly talked

one square of light on the wall waiting patiently

I will learn my multiplication tables

while the woman in the old photograph looks in a different direction

Up-Hill

Does the road wind up-hill all the way?
  Yes, to the very end.
Will the day's journey take the whole long day?
  From morn to night, my friend.

But is there for the night a resting-place?
  A roof for when the slow dark hours begin.
May not the darkness hide it from my face?
  You cannot miss that inn.

Shall I meet other wayfarers at night?
  Those who have gone before.
Then must I knock, or call when just in sight?
  They will not keep you standing at that door.

Shall I find comfort, travel-sore and weak?
  Of labour you shall find the sum.
Will there be beds for me and all who seek?
  Yea, beds for all who come.

LAURENCE ALMA-TADEMA
(1836–1912)

Playgrounds

In summer I am very glad
We children are so small,
For we can see a thousand things
That men can't see at all.

They don't know much about the moss
And all the stones they pass:
They never lie and play among
The forests in the grass:

They walk about a long way off;
And, when we're at the sea,
Let father stoop as best he can
He can't find things like me.

But, when the snow is on the ground
And all the puddles freeze,
I wish that I were very tall,
High up above the trees . . .

MAURYA SIMON
(1950–)

The Fishermen at Guasti Park

In the first days of summer
the three elms, those slightly
opened fans, unfold
their shadows across the river.
Two dogs arrive exhausted,
tongues dripping, and settle
down near the frogbait jars.
Aiming their poles
toward the center of water,
the Sunday fishermen watch
the light pirouette off
the opposite shore.
Their wives peel onions,
open wine, do their nails.
Most of the men think
as little about gravity
as they do about war and
the weightlessness of time.
How could they know that
it is only the single, collective
thought of their abandoned childhoods
that keeps the world afloat?

RANDALL MANN
(1972–)

Poem Beginning with a Line by John Ashbery

Jealousy. Whispered weather reports.
The lure of the land so strong it prompts
gossip: we chatter like small birds
at the edge of the ocean gray, foaming.

Now sand under sand hides
the buried world, the one in which our fathers failed,
the palm frond a dangerous truth
they once believed, and touched. Bloodied their hands.

They once believed. And, touched, bloodied their hands;
the palm frond, a dangerous truth;
the buried world, the one in which our fathers failed.
Now sand under sand hides

at the edge of the ocean: gray, foaming
gossip. We chatter like small birds,
the lure of the land so strong it prompts
jealousy. Whispered weather reports.

MARK IRWIN
(1953–)

My Father's Hats

Sunday mornings I would reach
high into his dark closet while standing
    on a chair and tiptoeing reach
higher, touching, sometimes fumbling
    the soft crowns and imagine
I was in a forest, wind hymning
    through pines, where the musky scent
of rain clinging to damp earth was
    his scent I loved, lingering on
bands, leather, and on the inner silk
    crowns where I would smell his
hair and almost think I was being
    held, or climbing a tree, touching
the yellow fruit, leaves whose scent
    was that of clove in the godsome
air, as now, thinking of his fabulous
    sleep, I stand on this canyon floor
and watch light slowly close
    on water I'm not sure is there.

PAUL LAURENCE DUNBAR
(1872–1906)

Beyond the Years

I

Beyond the years the answer lies,
Beyond where brood the grieving skies
   And Night drops tears.
Where Faith rod-chastened smiles to rise
   And doff its fears,
And carping Sorrow pines and dies—
   Beyond the years.

II

Beyond the years the prayer for rest
Shall beat no more within the breast;
   The darkness clears,
And Morn perched on the mountain's crest
   Her form uprears—
The day that is to come is best,
   Beyond the years.

III

Beyond the years the soul shall find
That endless peace for which it pined,
   For light appears,
And to the eyes that still were blind
   With blood and tears,
Their sight shall come all unconfined
   Beyond the years.

SHERMAN ALEXIE
(1966–)

Dangerous Astronomy

I wanted to walk outside and praise the stars,
But David, my baby son, coughed and coughed.
His comfort was more important than the stars

So I comforted and kissed him in his dark
Bedroom, but my comfort was not enough.
His mother was more important than the stars

So he cried for her breast and milk. It's hard
For fathers to compete with mothers' love.
In the dark, mothers illuminate like the stars!

Dull and jealous, I was the smallest part
Of the whole. I know this is stupid stuff
But I felt less important than the farthest star

As my wife fed my son in the hungry dark.
How can a father resent his son and his son's love?
Was my comfort more important than the stars?

A selfish father, I wanted to pull apart
My comfortable wife and son. Forgive me, Rough
God, because I walked outside and praised the stars,
And thought I was more important than the stars.

C. D. WRIGHT
(1949–)

Imaginary June

for Susie Schlesinger

Night: wears itself away   clouds too dense to skim
over the shear granite rim   only a moment before
someone sitting in a mission chair   convinced 101%
convinced   she could see into her very cells
with her unassisted eyes   even into extremophiles
even with the light dispelled   until the mind sets sail
into its private interval of oblivion   a hand falls from its lap
a pen drops to a carpet   a stand of leaves whispers as if
to suggest something tender   yet potentially heart robbing

Sequel: to a dream in which faces flare up   fuse   dissolve
but there is a lot of color before their vanishing   and a name
for such phenomena   that comes from the belly of a lamb
rather   not a lamb anymore   from the stomach
of a particular canny but kind and   blind-from-birth ewe

NATHAN HOKS
(1977–)

Toy Cloud

The rabbit has stolen
The big bear's pointy red hat.

The frog looks longingly
At its evaporating pond.

A powerful glow comes
Off the sunflower

So everyone wears goggles.
My son rolls around in the ferns.

It seems he has overdosed
On sugar cookies.

Does he care about the bear's hat?
To him I am a ghost on a bicycle.

I remember my father's mouth
Reading aloud beneath his beard.

He is hiding in my face.
The toy cloud is filled with rain.

We Real Cool

The Pool Players.
Seven at the Golden Shovel.

We real cool. We
Left school. We

Lurk late. We
Strike straight. We

Sing sin. We
Thin gin. We

Jazz June. We
Die soon.

DAWN LUNDY MARTIN
(1968–)

from Disciplines

This is how much fortuitiveness weighs. Measure in dirt. Of vices and
other habits. Of leaving a house at 3 am and drawn as would any tether
and here is your lock, my dear. I want to say this plainly: it is only when
I am in a woman's arms that my body is not a threat. Neither crosses nor
damnation. Fix nor flutter. Hangs here, this balance, and one opens the
car door and drives along the river where it said a crossing might happen.
Had happened. Many times. Sticklers will say, not here. There are no
crossings here. But, there the I is, reflection and delivered, on the other
side. Like hams, holding on to what was.

GEORGE MOSES HORTON
(1797–1883)

The Graduate
Leaving College

What summons do I hear?
　The morning peal, departure's knell;
My eyes let fall a friendly tear,
　And bid this place farewell.

Attending servants come,
　The carriage wheels like thunders roar,
To bear the pensive seniors home,
　Here to be seen no more.

Pass one more transient night,
　The morning sweeps the College clean;
The graduate takes his last long flight,
　No more in College seen.

The bee, in which courts the flower,
　Must with some pain itself employ,
And then fly, at the day's last hour,
　Home to its hive with joy.

MARK YAKICH
(1970–)

Troubadour

When I was a boy and my fist
Would land into my father's arm,

I'd cry out, and he'd say
Didn't hurt me none.

He's been dead six years now,
And my work is still to try

To beat myself up
And make the pain last.

ADA LIMÓN
(1976–)

Before

No shoes and a glossy
red helmet, I rode
on the back of my dad's
Harley at seven years old.
Before the divorce.
Before the new apartment.
Before the new marriage.
Before the apple tree.
Before the ceramics in the garbage.
Before the dog's chain.
Before the koi were all eaten
by the crane. Before the road
between us, there was the road
beneath us, and I was just
big enough not to let go:
Henno Road, creek just below,
rough wind, chicken legs,
and I never knew survival
was like that. If you live,
you look back and beg
for it again, the hazardous
bliss before you know
what you would miss.

EDGAR GUEST
(1881–1959)

Only a Dad

Only a dad with a tired face,
Coming home from the daily race,
Bringing little of gold or fame
To show how well he has played the game;
But glad in his heart that his own rejoice
To see him come and to hear his voice.

Only a dad with a brood of four,
One of ten million men or more
Plodding along in the daily strife,
Bearing the whips and the scorns of life,
With never a whimper of pain or hate,
For the sake of those who at home await.

Only a dad, neither rich nor proud,
Merely one of the surging crowd,
Toiling, striving from day to day,
Facing whatever may come his way,
Silent whenever the harsh condemn,
And bearing it all for the love of them.

Only a dad but he gives his all
To smooth the way for his children small,
Doing with courage stern and grim,
The deeds that his father did for him.
This is the line that for him I pen:
Only a dad, but the best of men.

To Her Father, with Some Verses

Most truly honored, and as truly dear,
If worth in me or aught I do appear,
Who can of right better demand the same
Than may your worthy self, from whom it came?
The principal might yield a greater sum,
Yet, handled ill, amounts but to this crumb.
My stock's so small I know not how to pay,
My bond remains in force unto this day;
Yet for part payment take this simple mite.
Where nothing's to be had kings lose their right.
Such is my debt I may not say "Forgive!"
But as I can I'll pay it while I live;
Such is my bond none can discharge but I,
Yet, paying, is not paid until I die.

GEFFREY DAVIS
(1983–)

The Epistemology
of Cheerios

this the week of our son's first
upright wobble from kitchen

to living-room   and he begins planting
tiny Os wherever his fleshy fingers

can reach   each first shelf   each chair
cushion   each pair of shoes   he goes

to bury a piece behind the TV
inside the pool of exposed wires

we've been saving him from
since he took to motion   and I let him

go for it   he survives   but why
this risk   how costly this whole-

grain crumb   back from
the wilderness of worry   for whom

Resignation

I like trees because they seem more resigned
to the way they have to live than other things do.
—Willa Cather

Here the oak and silver-breasted birches
Stand in their sweet familiarity
While underground, as in a black mirror,
They have concealed their tangled grievances,
Identical to the branching calm above
But there ensnared, each with the others' hold
On what gives life to which is brutal enough.
Still, in the air, none tries to keep company
Or change its fortune. They seem to lean
On the light, unconcerned with what the world
Makes of their decencies, and will not show
A jealous purchase on their length of days.
To never having been loved as they wanted
Or deserved, to anyone's sudden infatuation
Gouged into their sides, to all they are forced
To shelter and to hide, they have resigned themselves.

EDNA ST. VINCENT MILLAY
(1892–1950)

I know I am but summer to your heart (Sonnet XXVII)

I know I am but summer to your heart,
And not the full four seasons of the year;
And you must welcome from another part
Such noble moods as are not mine, my dear.
No gracious weight of golden fruits to sell
Have I, nor any wise and wintry thing;
And I have loved you all too long and well
To carry still the high sweet breast of Spring.
Wherefore I say: O love, as summer goes,
I must be gone, steal forth with silent drums,
That you may hail anew the bird and rose
When I come back to you, as summer comes.
Else will you seek, at some not distant time,
Even your summer in another clime.

Camp of No Return

I sat in the old tree swing without swinging. My loafer had fallen off and I left it on the ground. My sister came running out of the house to tell me something. She said, "I'm going to camp tomorrow." I said, "I don't believe you." She said, "I am. It's a fact. Mother told me." We didn't speak for the rest of the day. I was mad at her for getting to do something I didn't. At dinner I asked mother what kind of camp it was. She said, "Oh, just a camp like any other." I didn't really know what that meant. The next day they got her ready to go, and then they drove off, leaving me with the neighbors. When they got back everything was normal, except I missed Maisie. And I missed her more each following day. I didn't know how much she had meant to me before. I asked my parents over and over how much longer it would be. All they said was soon. I told some kids at school how long my sister had been gone. One of them said, "She'll never be back. That's the death camp." When I got home I told my parents what that boy had said. "He doesn't know what he's talking about," my father said. But after a couple of more weeks of her absence I began to wonder. That's when they began to clean out Maisie's room. I said, "What are you doing? You said Maisie will be back soon." My mother said, "Maisie's not coming back. She likes it there better than she does here." "That's not true. I don't believe you," I said. My father gave me a look that let me know I might be next if I didn't mend my ways. I never said a word about Maisie again.

SARA TEASDALE
(1884–1933)

Summer Night, Riverside

In the wild soft summer darkness
How many and many a night we two together
Sat in the park and watched the Hudson
Wearing her lights like golden spangles
Glinting on black satin.
The rail along the curving pathway
Was low in a happy place to let us cross,
And down the hill a tree that dripped with bloom
Sheltered us,
While your kisses and the flowers,
Falling, falling,
Tangled my hair . . . .

The frail white stars moved slowly over the sky.

And now, far off
In the fragrant darkness
The tree is tremulous again with bloom
For June comes back.

To-night what girl
When she goes home,
Dreamily before her mirror shakes from her hair
This year's blossoms, clinging in its coils?

CARL SANDBURG
(1878–1967)

Summer Stars

Bend low again, night of summer stars.
So near you are, sky of summer stars,
So near, a long arm man can pick off stars,
Pick off what he wants in the sky bowl,
So near you are, summer stars,
So near, strumming, strumming,
　　　So lazy and hum-strumming.

GEORGIA DOUGLAS JOHNSON
(1880–1966)

When I Rise Up

When I rise up above the earth,
And look down on the things that fetter me,
I beat my wings upon the air,
Or tranquil lie,
Surge after surge of potent strength
Like incense comes to me
When I rise up above the earth
And look down upon the things that fetter me.

RICHARD WILBUR
(1921–)

June Light

Your voice, with clear location of June days,
Called me—outside the window. You were there,
Light yet composed, as in the just soft stare
Of uncontested summer all things raise
Plainly their seeming into seamless air.

Then your love looked as simple and entire
As that picked pear you tossed me, and your face
As legible as pearskin's fleck and trace,
Which promise always wine, by mottled fire
More fatal fleshed than ever human grace.

And your gay gift—Oh when I saw it fall
Into my hands, through all that naïve light,
It seemed as blessed with truth and new delight
As must have been the first great gift of all.

SUZANNE RANCOURT
(1959–)

Whose Mouth Do I Speak With

I can remember my father bringing home spruce gum.
He worked in the woods and filled his pockets
with golden chunks of pitch.
For his children
he provided this special sacrament
and we'd gather at this feet, around his legs,
bumping his lunchbox, and his empty thermos rattled inside.
Our skin would stick to Daddy's gluey clothing
and we'd smell like Mumma's Pine Sol.
We had no money for store bought gum
but that's all right.
The spruce gum
was so close to chewing amber
as though in our mouths we held the eyes of Coyote
and how many other children had fathers
that placed on their innocent, anxious tongue
the blood of tree?

Admission

Victor Hugo claimed that *the dream*
is the aquarium of the night

confirming for the tourist
the mysterious hush

when viewing the depths sealed behind plate glass.
Even more than dream, I wish

to name the various species;
to stare or flee the one that sports a playmate's face

blinking back at me. Cathedral of science!
Cathedral of childhood! Of childhood nights!

Of adult—what? Of remorse as a hall
to which we pay admission?

Ithaca

I've been blessed
with a few gusts of wind,
a few loves
to wave goodbye to.
I still think of mother's kitchen,
sorry for tantrums
of way back when. No frost
lodged in me then. In those days
snow spread through town
like an epidemic: how archival
the blankness seemed.
If you flew above
the shell of the old house
it was nothing really:
there was no story
to our little ranch house,
so you couldn't hear a thing.

ARCHIBALD MACLEISH
(1892–1982)

Imagery

The tremulously mirrored clouds lie deep,
Enchanted towers bosomed in the stream,
And blossomed coronals of white-thorn gleam
Within the water where the willows sleep—
Still-imaged willow-leaves whose shadows steep
The far-reflected sky in dark of dream;
And glimpsed therein the sun-winged swallows seem
As fleeting memories to those who weep.

So mirrored in thy heart are all desires,
Eternal longings, Youth's inheritance,
All hopes that token immortality,
All griefs whereto immortal grief aspires.
Aweary of the world's reality,
I dream above the imaged pool, Romance.

IDRA NOVEY
(1978–)

Still Life with Invisible Canoe

Levinas asked if we have the right
To be   the way I ask my sons
If they'd like to be trees

The way the word tree
Makes them a little animal
Dancing up and down
Like bears in movies

Bears I have to say
Pretend we are children

At a river one of them says
So we sip it   pivot in the hallway
Call it a canoe

It is noon in the living room
We are rowing through a blue
That is a feeling mostly

The way drifting greenly
Under real trees
Is a feeling near holy

July

BRYNN SAITO
(1981–)

Like Any Good American

I bathe my television   in total attention   I give it my corneas
I give it my eardrums   I give it my longing
In return I get pictures   of girls fighting   and men flying
and women in big houses   with tight faces   blotting down tears
with tiny knuckles   Sometimes my mother calls
and I don't answer   Sometimes a siren   sings past the window
and summer air   pushes in   dripping with the scent
of human sweat   But what do I care   I've given my skin
to the TV   I've given it my tastes   In return   it gives me so many
different sounds   to fill the silence   where the secrets
of my life   flash by like ad space   for the coming season

WALT WHITMAN
(1819–1892)

I Hear America Singing

I hear America singing, the varied carols I hear,
Those of mechanics, each one singing his as it should be blithe and
    strong,
The carpenter singing his as he measures his plank or beam,
The mason singing his as he makes ready for work, or leaves off work,
The boatman singing what belongs to him in his boat, the deckhand
    singing on the steamboat deck,
The shoemaker singing as he sits on his bench, the hatter singing as he
    stands,
The wood-cutter's song, the ploughboy's on his way in the morning, or at
    noon intermission or at sundown,
The delicious singing of the mother, or of the young wife at work, or of
    the girl sewing or washing,
Each singing what belongs to him or her and to none else,
The day what belongs to the day—at night the party of young fellows,
    robust, friendly,
Singing with open mouths their strong melodious songs.

LANGSTON HUGHES
(1902–1967)

I, Too

I, too, sing America.

I am the darker brother.
They send me to eat in the kitchen
When company comes,
But I laugh,
And eat well,
And grow strong.

Tomorrow,
I'll be at the table
When company comes.
Nobody'll dare
Say to me,
"Eat in the kitchen,"
Then.

Besides,
They'll see how beautiful I am
And be ashamed—

I, too, am America.

ROBERT CREELEY
(1926–2005)

America

America, you ode for reality!
Give back the people you took.

Let the sun shine again
on the four corners of the world

you thought of first but do not
own, or keep like a convenience.

People are your own word, you
invented that locus and term.

Here, you said and say, is
where we are. Give back

what we are, these people you made,
us, and nowhere but you to be.

CLAUDE MCKAY
(1889–1948)

America

Although she feeds me bread of bitterness,
And sinks into my throat her tiger's tooth,
Stealing my breath of life, I will confess
I love this cultured hell that tests my youth!
Her vigor flows like tides into my blood,
Giving me strength erect against her hate.
Her bigness sweeps my being like a flood.
Yet as a rebel fronts a king in state,
I stand within her walls with not a shred
Of terror, malice, not a word of jeer.
Darkly I gaze into the days ahead,
And see her might and granite wonders there,
Beneath the touch of Time's unerring hand,
Like priceless treasures sinking in the sand.

JOSEPH LEASE
(1960–)

America

Try saying *wren*.

It's midnight

in my body, 4 a.m. in my body, breading and olives and
cherries. Wait, it's all rotten. How am I ever. Oh notebook.
A clown explains the war. What start or color or kind of
grace. I have to teach. I have to run, eat less junk. Oh CNN.
What start or color. There's a fist of meat in my solar plexus
and green light in my mouth and little chips of dream flake
off my skin. Try saying *wren*. Try saying
mercy.

Try anything.

NOELLE KOCOT
(1969–)

The Peace That So Lovingly Descends

"You" have transformed into "my loss."
The nettles in your vanished hair
Restore the absolute truth
Of warring animals without a haven.
I know, I'm as pathetic as a railroad
Without tracks. In June, I eat
The lonesome berries from the branches.
What can I say, except the forecast
Never changes. I sleep without you,
And the letters that you sent
Are now faded into failed lessons
Of an animal that's found a home. This.

SHARON OLDS
(1942–)

When

I wonder, now, only when it will happen,
when the young mother will hear the
noise like somebody's pressure cooker
down the block, going off. She'll go out in the yard,
holding her small daughter in her arms,
and there, above the end of the street, in the
air above the line of the trees,
she will see it rising, lifting up
over our horizon, the upper rim of the
gold ball, large as a giant
planet starting to lift up over ours.
She will stand there in the yard holding her daughter,
looking at it rise and glow and blossom and rise,
and the child will open her arms to it,
it will look so beautiful.

MARIANNE MOORE
(1887–1972)

Ennui

He often expressed
A curious wish,
To be interchangeably
Man and fish;
To nibble the bait
Off the hook,
Said he,
And then slip away
Like a ghost
In the sea.

RANDALL JARRELL
(1914–1965)

Eighth Air Force

If, in an odd angle of the hutment,
A puppy laps the water from a can
Of flowers, and the drunk sergeant shaving
Whistles O Paradiso!—shall I say that man
Is not as men have said: a wolf to man?

The other murderers troop in yawning;
Three of them play Pitch, one sleeps, and one
Lies counting missions, lies there sweating
Till even his heart beats: One; One; One.
O murderers! . . . Still, this is how it's done:

This is a war. . . . But since these play, before they die,
Like puppies with their puppy; since, a man,
I did as these have done, but did not die—
I will content the people as I can
And give up these to them: Behold the man!

I have suffered, in a dream, because of him,
Many things; for this last saviour, man,
I have lied as I lie now. But what is lying?
Men wash their hands, in blood, as best they can:
I find no fault in this just man.

TRACY K. SMITH
(1972–)

Sci-Fi

There will be no edges, but curves.
Clean lines pointing only forward.

History, with its hard spine & dog-eared
Corners, will be replaced with nuance,

Just like the dinosaurs gave way
To mounds and mounds of ice.

Women will still be women, but
The distinction will be empty. Sex,

Having outlived every threat, will gratify
Only the mind, which is where it will exist.

For kicks, we'll dance for ourselves
Before mirrors studded with golden bulbs.

The oldest among us will recognize that glow—
But the word sun will have been re-assigned

To a Standard Uranium-Neutralizing device
Found in households and nursing homes.

And yes, we'll live to be much older, thanks
To popular consensus. Weightless, unhinged,

Eons from even our own moon, we'll drift
In the haze of space, which will be, once

And for all, scrutable and safe.

EMMA LAZARUS
(1849–1887)

The New Colossus

Not like the brazen giant of Greek fame,
With conquering limbs astride from land to land;
Here at our sea-washed, sunset gates shall stand
A mighty woman with a torch, whose flame
Is the imprisoned lightning, and her name
Mother of Exiles. From her beacon-hand
Glows world-wide welcome; her mild eyes command
The air-bridged harbor that twin cities frame.
"Keep, ancient lands, your storied pomp!" cries she
With silent lips. "Give me your tired, your poor,
Your huddled masses yearning to breathe free,
The wretched refuse of your teeming shore.
Send these, the homeless, tempest-tost to me,
I lift my lamp beside the golden door!"

MAJOR JACKSON
(1968–)

Life During Wartime

But the daydream collapses and time returns us
to corners where young boys expire
like comets at the suburbs of your thalamus.
Gunshots weaken the houses; hope vanishes
like old cell phones. Blood darkens a stoop;
the mouth is disagreeable. But then, one afternoon,
a sunshower baptizes shadows on a street. The steaming
scent of wet sidewalks swells your insides,
and somewhere not far from here a young girl grabs
the hand of a boy and runs over the rubble.

JAMES MERRILL
(1926–1995)

A Dedication

Hans, there are moments when the whole mind
Resolves into a pair of brimming eyes, or lips
Parting to drink from the deep spring of a death
That freshness they do not yet need to understand.
These are the moments, if ever, an angel steps
Into the mind, as kings into the dress
Of a poor goatherd, for their acts of charity.
There are moments when speech is but a mouth pressed
Lightly and humbly against the angel's hand.

JO SARZOTTI
(1948–)

Horse Latitudes

The past lies in the brine
            Of equatorial water,
Parchment-folded,
Black ink veining where the quill paused.

Rich doldrums
            Full of gold
Where Spanish sailors
            Threw the Queen's horses,
Palomino, the color of her hair.

On the Outer Banks
            Each wave a breaking
Promise of the New World,
            Lost colonies,
Lost ships, wild ponies
                        Swimming even now.

AI
(1947–2010)

The Root Eater

The war has begun
and I see the Root Eater bending,
shifting his hands under the soil
in search of the arthritic knuckles of trees.
I see dazed flower stems
pushing themselves back into the ground.
I see turnips spinning endlessly
on the blunt, bitten-off tips of their noses.
I see the Root Eater going home on his knees,
full of the ripe foundations of things,
longing to send his seed up through his feet
and out into the morning

but the stumps of trees heave themselves forward
for the last march
and the Root Eater waits,
knowing he will be shoved, rootless,
under the brown, scaly torso of the rock.

JEHANNE DUBROW
(1975–)

The Long Deployment

For weeks, I breathe his body in the sheet
    and pillow. I lift a blanket to my face.
There's bitter incense paired with something sweet,
    like sandalwood left sitting in the heat
or cardamom rubbed on a piece of lace.
    For weeks, I breathe his body. In the sheet
I smell anise, the musk that we secrete
    with longing, leather and moss. I find a trace
of bitter incense paired with something sweet.
    Am I imagining the wet scent of peat
and cedar, oud, impossible to erase?
    For weeks, I breathe his body in the sheet—
crushed pepper—although perhaps discreet,
    difficult for someone else to place.
There's bitter incense paired with something sweet.
    With each deployment I become an aesthete
of smoke and oak. Patchouli fills the space
    for weeks. I breathe his body in the sheet
until he starts to fade, made incomplete,
    a bottle almost empty in its case.
There's bitter incense paired with something sweet.
    And then he's gone. Not even the conceit
of him remains, not the resinous base.
    For weeks, I breathed his body in the sheet.
He was bitter incense paired with something sweet.

AIMEE NEZHUKUMATATHIL
(1974–)

Upon Hearing the News
You Buried Our Dog

I have faith in the single glossy capsule of a butterfly egg.
I have faith in the way a wasp nest is never quiet

and never wants to be. I have faith that the pile of forty
painted turtles balanced on top of each other will not fall

as the whole messy mass makes a scrabble-run
for the creek and away from a fox's muddy paws.

I have been thinking of you on these moonless nights—
nights so full of blue fur and needle-whiskers, I don't dare

linger outside for long. I wonder if scientists could classify
us a binary star—something like *Albireo*, four-hundred

light years away. I love that this star is actually two—
one blue, one gold, circling each other, never touching—

a single star soldered and edged in two colors if you spy it
on a clear night in July. And if this evening, wherever you are,

brings you face to face with a raccoon or possum—
be careful of the teeth and all that wet bite.

During the darkest part of the night, teeth grow longer
in their mouths. And if the oleander spins you still

another way—take a turn and follow it. It will help you avoid
the spun-light sky, what singularity we might've become.

KRISTY BOWEN
(1974–)

house of strays

Suddenly, a hole opens in the year and we slip into it, the riptide
pull of strange, lonely dogs and broken phone lines.
You forgive me if I mistake *hunted* for *haunted*,
but I do like to rearrange things in my body every few years.
Take a can of gasoline to the frayed and ghosted.
Lights out. All hands on deck.
Still you wonder why I keep losing my shoes in the road
and coaxing cats in the alley with cans of tunafish and a flashlight.
Why my contentment is beautiful, but highly improbable, sort of like
four leaf clovers or an ice cream truck in the middle of the night.
This tiny thing breathing between us that aches something awful.
By summer, I am slipping all the complimentary mints in my coat pockets
while you pay the check. Gripping the railings on bridges to keep
diving over. Some dark dog in my throat when I say *hello*.

EDWARD HIRSCH
(1950–)

Veterans of Foreign Wars

Let's not forget the General
Shuffling out in his gray slippers
To feed the pigeons in Logan Square.

He wore a battered White Sox cap
And a heavy woolen scarf tossed
Over his shoulder, even in summer.

I remember how he muttered to himself
And coughed into his newspaper
And complained about his gout

To the other Latvian exiles,
The physicist who lived on Gogol Street
In Riga, my grandfather's hometown,

The auxiliary policeman from Daugavpils,
And the chemical engineer,
Who always gave me hard candy,

Though grandfather spit
And grandmother hurried me away
When she saw them coming.

WILLIAM CULLEN BRYANT
(1794–1878)

Midsummer

A power is on the earth and in the air
 From which the vital spirit shrinks afraid,
 And shelters him, in nooks of deepest shade,
From the hot steam and from the fiery glare.
Look forth upon the earth—her thousand plants
 Are smitten; even the dark sun-loving maize
 Faints in the field beneath the torrid blaze;
The herd beside the shaded fountain pants;
For life is driven from all the landscape brown;
 The bird has sought his tree, the snake his den,
 The trout floats dead in the hot stream, and men
Drop by the sun-stroke in the populous town;
 As if the Day of Fire had dawned, and sent
 Its deadly breath into the firmament.

After David Hammons

In the darkened moment a body gifted with the blue light of a flashlight
enters with levity, with or without assumptions, doubts, with desire,
the beating heart, disappointment, with desires—

Stand where you are.

You begin to move around in search of the steps it will take before you
are thrown back into your own body, back into your own need to be found.

Destinations are lost. You raise yourself. No one else is seeking.

You exhaust yourself looking into the blue light. All day blue burrows
the atmosphere. What doesn't belong with you won't be seen.

You could build a world out of need or you could hold everything
back and see. You could hold everything back. You hold back the black.

You hold everything black. You hold this body's lack. You hold yourself
back until nothing's left but the dissolving blues of metaphor.

HOWARD ALTMANN
(1963–)

Holding Posture

History sits on a chair
in a room without windows.
Mornings it searches for a door,
afternoons it naps.
At the stroke of midnight,
it stretches its body and sighs.
It keeps time and loses time,
knows its place and doesn't know its place.
Sometimes it considers the chair a step,
sometimes it believes the chair is not there.
To corners it never looks the same.
Under a full moon it holds its own.
History sits on a chair
in a room above our houses.

DORIANNE LAUX
(1952–)

On the Back Porch

The cat calls for her dinner.
On the porch I bend and pour
brown soy stars into her bowl,
stroke her dark fur.
It's not quite night.
Pinpricks of light in the eastern sky.
Above my neighbor's roof, a transparent
moon, a pink rag of cloud.
Inside my house are those who love me.
My daughter dusts biscuit dough.
And there's a man who will lift my hair
in his hands, brush it
until it throws sparks.
Everything is just as I've left it.
Dinner simmers on the stove.
Glass bowls wait to be filled
with gold broth. Sprigs of parsley
on the cutting board.
I want to smell this rich soup, the air
around me going dark, as stars press
their simple shapes into the sky.
I want to stay on the back porch
while the world tilts
toward sleep, until what I love
misses me, and calls me in.

There Is Absolutely Nothing Lonelier

There is absolutely nothing lonelier
than the little Mars rover
never shutting down, digging up
rocks, so far away from Bond Street
in a light rain. I wonder
if he makes little beeps? If so
he is lonelier still. He fires a laser
into the dust. He coughs. A shiny
thing in the sand turns out to be his.

AMY LAWLESS
(1977–)

Inspire Hope

I am in a common despair. So in order for me to have hope, it is crucial
to stack fifty pounds of books on the left-hand side of my bed. I cover him
tightly with my warmest woolen blankets. This boyfriend is named Shiver.
He is best left alone to his thoughts. But one night, I will accidentally roll
into him. He'll fall on me with such grace and with the acceleration of all
of history.

LARRY LEVIS
(1946–1996)

In a Country

My love and I are inventing a country, which we can already see taking
shape, as if wheels were passing through yellow mud. But there is a
problem: if we put a river in the country, it will thaw and begin flooding.
If we put the river on the border, there will be trouble. If we forget about
the river, there will be no way out. There is already a sky over that country,
waiting for clouds or smoke. Birds have flown into it, too. Each evening
more trees fill with their eyes, and what they see we can never erase.

One day it was snowing heavily, and again we were lying in bed, watching
our country: we could make out the wide river for the first time, blue and
moving. We seemed to be getting closer; we saw our wheel tracks leading
into it and curving out of sight behind us. It looked like the land we had
left, some smoke in the distance, but I wasn't sure. There were birds
calling. The creaking of our wheels. And as we entered that country, it felt
as if someone was touching our bare shoulders, lightly, for the last time.

Wind in a Box

This ink. This name. This blood. This blunder.
This blood. This loss. This lonesome wind. This canyon.
This / twin / swiftly / paddling / shadow blooming
an inch above the carpet—. This cry. This mud.
This shudder. This is where I stood: by the bed,
by the door, by the window, in the night / in the night.
How deep, how often / must a woman be touched?
How deep, how often have I been touched?
On the bone, on the shoulder, on the brow, on the knuckle:
Touch like a last name, touch like a wet match.
Touch like an empty shoe and an empty shoe, sweet
and incomprehensible. This ink. This name. This blood
and wonder. This box. This body in a box. This blood
in the body. This wind in the blood.

GWENDOLYN BROOKS
(1917–2000)

the sonnet-ballad

Oh mother, mother, where is happiness?
They took my lover's tallness off to war,
Left me lamenting. Now I cannot guess
What I can use an empty heart-cup for.
He won't be coming back here any more.
Some day the war will end, but, oh, I knew
When he went walking grandly out that door
That my sweet love would have to be untrue.
Would have to be untrue. Would have to court
Coquettish death, whose impudent and strange
Possessive arms and beauty (of a sort)
Can make a hard man hesitate—and change.
And he will be the one to stammer, "Yes."
Oh mother, mother, where is happiness?

PHILIP LEVINE
(1928–2015)

Our Valley

We don't see the ocean, not ever, but in July and August
when the worst heat seems to rise from the hard clay
of this valley, you could be walking through a fig orchard
when suddenly the wind cools and for a moment
you get a whiff of salt, and in that moment you can almost
believe something is waiting beyond the Pacheco Pass,
something massive, irrational, and so powerful even
the mountains that rise east of here have no word for it.

You probably think I'm nuts saying the mountains
have no word for ocean, but if you live here
you begin to believe they know everything.
They maintain that huge silence we think of as divine,
a silence that grows in autumn when snow falls
slowly between the pines and the wind dies
to less than a whisper and you can barely catch
your breath because you're thrilled and terrified.

You have to remember this isn't your land.
It belongs to no one, like the sea you once lived beside
and thought was yours. Remember the small boats
that bobbed out as the waves rode in, and the men
who carved a living from it only to find themselves
carved down to nothing. Now you say this is home,
so go ahead, worship the mountains as they dissolve in dust,
wait on the wind, catch a scent of salt, call it our life.

JEFFREY BROWN
(1956–)

History

At a clearer time
from a greater distance
when the confusion has faded
the battle long done
the lies cut down like
wheat in late summer
in this very field
of human harvests—

then you will know
what happened here
you, so frightened now
and you, so fearsome.

August

Vacation

I love the hour before takeoff,
that stretch of no time, no home
but the gray vinyl seats linked like
unfolding paper dolls. Soon we shall
be summoned to the gate, soon enough
there'll be the clumsy procedure of row numbers
and perforated stubs—but for now
I can look at these ragtag nuclear families
with their cooing and bickering
or the heeled bachelorette trying
to ignore a baby's wail and the baby's
exhausted mother waiting to be called up early
while the athlete, one monstrous hand
asleep on his duffel bag, listens,
perched like a seal trained for the plunge.
Even the lone executive
who has wandered this far into summer
with his lasered itinerary, briefcase
knocking his knees—even he
has worked for the pleasure of bearing
no more than a scrap of himself
into this hall. He'll dine out, she'll sleep late,
they'll let the sun burn them happy all morning
—a little hope, a little whimsy
before the loudspeaker blurts
and we leap up to become
Flight 828, now boarding at Gate 17.

KAY RYAN
(1945–)

Home to Roost

The chickens
are circling and
blotting out the
day. The sun is
bright, but the
chickens are in
the way. Yes,
the sky is dark
with chickens,
dense with them.
They turn and
then they turn
again. These
are the chickens
you let loose
one at a time
and small—
various breeds.
Now they have
come home
to roost—all
the same kind
at the same speed.

BRENDA SHAUGHNESSY
(1970–)

Mermaid's Purse

There is no such thing as sacrifice,
though the bleeding doesn't end.

The self is the self yet bigger than itself.
Indebted. And subordinate

to the unity of its fragments,
loopholes in the loop of wholeness.

Cat sharks lay their eggsacs,
which eat themselves in gestation,

for if fewer mature sharks,
bigger portions at the feast

of the loggerhead turtle, which
will never again be a single entity.

Out of one, many. If blameless,
then meaningless, dissolved

by a cloud of sardines, flashing
silver as if paying for breakfast

in a silent movie starring no stars.

CARL SANDBURG
(1878–1967)

Window

Night from a railroad car window
Is a great, dark, soft thing
Broken across with slashes of light.

Travelling

This is the spot:—how mildly does the sun
Shine in between the fading leaves! the air
In the habitual silence of this wood
Is more than silent: and this bed of heath,
Where shall we find so sweet a resting-place?
Come!—let me see thee sink into a dream
Of quiet thoughts,—protracted till thine eye
Be calm as water when the winds are gone
And no one can tell whither.—my sweet friend!
We two have had such happy hours together
That my heart melts in me to think of it.

LINDA PASTAN
(1932–)

Traveling Light

I'm only leaving you
for a handful of days,
but it feels as though
I'll be gone forever—
the way the door closes

behind me with such solidity,
the way my suitcase
carries everything
I'd need for an eternity
of traveling light.

I've left my hotel number
on your desk, instructions
about the dog
and heating dinner. But
like the weather front

they warn is on its way
with its switchblades
of wind and ice,
our lives have minds
of their own.

AFAA MICHAEL WEAVER
(1951–)

Unspoken

I saw my faith
riding on the light
in the ocean one
morning when
the sound of waves
breaking broke me,
I knew the weight
of what is too much
to try to see, each
sparkle in the light
the infinite space
inside the invisible
that lives in me and
will not surrender
itself to naming.

MATTHEW HENRIKSEN
(1977–)

The Bus through
Jonesboro, Arkansas

Inanimate intimacy in the plural
Couples under their dark covers

The distance between one body and another
An echo chamber against every stone

The distance between lovers in a rock-lashing wave
The solitude of two together under the waters of night

Or the flattened space between two people on a bus
Talking above the low beams of a few lost trucks

Seeking their destruction or their portion elsewhere
A road imagined as a slick for words in a discrete stream

Flawless enamel the tongue slides along
Or skates off into a future illumined within a highway sign

At the lip of revelation comes denouement or slow torturous sleep
Because traveling does not follow music

Only music brings the body down from the sky
The solid body in its partial form

EDNA ST. VINCENT MILLAY
(1892–1950)

Travel

The railroad track is miles away,
  And the day is loud with voices speaking,
Yet there isn't a train goes by all day
  But I hear its whistle shrieking.

All night there isn't a train goes by,
  Though the night is still for sleep and dreaming,
But I see its cinders red on the sky,
  And hear its engine steaming.

My heart is warm with the friends I make,
  And better friends I'll not be knowing;
Yet there isn't a train I wouldn't take,
  No matter where it's going.

JUAN FELIPE HERRERA
(1948–)

tomorrow I leave to
El Paso, Texas

see my brother-in-law with a styled shirt

in spite of his cancer below

then a small dinner in the evening the next day

no one knows except I may be on the road

Mesquite where my father settled in '31

forty-five minutes west then a left you go in

sister Sarita waits for me on Abby Street

after decades in separate families we just met

now I hear the clock snap I swipe an ant

time to walk my dogs five blocks and back

a different route to soothe the mind

it is the same one but I am hopeful

SHERWOOD ANDERSON
(1876–1941)

Evening Song

My song will rest while I rest. I struggle along. I'll get back to the corn
and the open fields. Don't fret, love, I'll come out all right.

Back of Chicago the open fields. Were you ever there—trains coming
toward you out of the East—streaks of light on the long gray plains?
Many a song—aching to sing.

I've got a gray and ragged brother in my breast—that's a fact. Back
of Chicago the open fields—long trains go west too—in the silence.
Don't fret, love. I'll come out all right.

CAROLYN FORCHÉ
(1950–)

Poem for Maya

Dipping our bread in oil tins
we talked of morning peeling
open our rooms to a moment
of almonds, olives and wind
when we did not yet know what we were.
The days in Mallorca were alike:
footprints down goat-paths
from the beds we had left,
at night the stars locked to darkness.
At that time we were learning
to dance, take our clothes
in our fingers and open
ourselves to their hands.
The *veranera* was with us.
For a month the almond trees bloomed,
their droppings the delicate silks
we removed when each time a touch
took us closer to the window where
we whispered *yes*, there on the intricate
balconies of breath, overlooking
the rest of our lives.

LANGSTON HUGHES
(1902–1967)

Dream Variations

To fling my arms wide
In some place of the sun,
To whirl and to dance
Till the white day is done.
Then rest at cool evening
Beneath a tall tree
While night comes on gently,
    Dark like me—
That is my dream!

To fling my arms wide
In the face of the sun,
Dance! Whirl! Whirl!
Till the quick day is done.
Rest at pale evening . . .
A tall, slim tree . . .
Night coming tenderly
    Black like me.

LAURIE SHECK
(1953–)

And water lies plainly

Then I came to an edge of very calm
  But couldn't stay there. It was the washed greenblue mapmakers use to
                                 indicate
Inlets and coves, softbroken contours where the land leaves off
  And water lies plainly, as if lamped by its own justice. I hardly know
                           how to say how it was
Though it spoke to me most kindly,
  Unlike a hard afterwards or the motions of forestalling.

Now in evening light the far-off ridge carries marks of burning.
  Below, the hills turn thundercolored, and my thoughts move toward
                         them, rough skins
Without their bodies. What is the part of us that feels it isn't named, that
                         doesn't know
  How to respond to any name? That scarcely or not at all can lift its head
Into the blue and so unfold there?

EMMA LAZARUS
(1849–1887)

Long Island Sound

I see it as it looked one afternoon
In August,—by a fresh soft breeze o'erblown.
The swiftness of the tide, the light thereon,
A far-off sail, white as a crescent moon.
The shining waters with pale currents strewn,
The quiet fishing-smacks, the Eastern cove,
The semi-circle of its dark, green grove.
The luminous grasses, and the merry sun
In the grave sky; the sparkle far and wide,
Laughter of unseen children, cheerful chirp
Of crickets, and low lisp of rippling tide,
Light summer clouds fantastical as sleep
Changing unnoted while I gazed thereon.
All these fair sounds and sights I made my own.

MARIE HOWE
(1950–)

The Dream

I had a dream in the day:
I laid my father's body down in a narrow boat

and sent him off along the riverbank with its cattails and grasses.
And the boat—it was made of bark and wood bent when it was wet—

took him to his burial finally.
But a day or two later I realized it was my self I wanted

to lay down, hands crossed, eyes closed. . . .
Oh, the light coming up from down there,

the sweet smell of the water—and finally, the sense of being carried
by a current I could not name or change.

JANE KENYON
(1947–1995)

Portrait of a Figure
Near Water

Rebuked, she turned and ran
uphill to the barn. Anger, the inner
arsonist, held a match to her brain.
She observed her life: against her will
it survived the unwavering flame.
The barn was empty of animals.
Only a swallow tilted
near the beams, and bats
hung from the rafters
the roof sagged between.
Her breath became steady
where, years past, the farmer cooled
the big tin amphoræ of milk.
The stone trough was still
filled with water: she watched it
and received its calm.
So it is when we retreat in anger:
we think we burn alone
and there is no balm.
Then water enters, though it makes
no sound.

NATHANIEL HAWTHORNE
(1804–1864)

The Ocean

The ocean hath its silent caves,
    Deep, quiet, and alone;
Though there be fury in the waves,
    Beneath them there is none.

The awful spirits of the deep,
    Hold their communion there;
And there are those for whom we weep,—
    The young, the bright, the fair.

Calmly the weary seamen rest,
    Beneath their own blue sea;
The ocean solitudes are blessed,
    For there is purity.

The earth has guilt, the earth has care,
    Unquiet are its graves;
But peaceful sleep is ever there,
    Beneath its dark blue waves.

Afterburn

Things too thin inhabit our dreams and we take on
their starving. We live until hunger

takes on such a shape that it is shoulder blades
in everything and sounds up in the trees. Then,

such ghosts. Such bones without skins doubled over.
A starless night every night and starlessness

is ashes or newsprint on the hands. Living
is barely a flock of birds the way it moves

like falling; it must be the cure for something,
the last lit house on a dead end street

or a hunger with two minds, drawing children
to the damp sheds at the far fence of their yards.

There is an entire August storm in everything said,
and to open the violent hives of remembering,

we imagine marigolds, birds drowned in the creek,
the lights left on in a room left behind.

LYNN EMANUEL
(1949–)

Sonnetesque

I love its smallness: as though our whole town
were a picture postcard and our feelings
were on vacation: ourselves in mini-
ature, shopping at tiny sales, buying
the newspapers—small and pale and square
as sugar cubes—at the fragile, little curb.
The way the streetlight is really a table
lamp where now we sit and where real
night, (which is very tall and black and
at our backs), where for a moment
the night is forced to bend down and look
through these tiny windows, forced to come
closer and put its hand on our shoulder
and stoop over the book to read the fine print.

ROBERT HASS
(1941–)

First Things at the Last Minute

The white water rush of some warbler's song.
Last night, a few strewings of ransacked moonlight
On the sheets. You don't know what slumped forward
In the nineteen-forties taxi or why they blamed you
Or what the altered landscape, willowy, riparian,
Had to do with the reasons why everyone
Should be giving things away, quickly,
Except for spendthrift sorrow that can't bear
The need to be forgiven and keeps looking for something
To forgive. The motion of washing machines
Is called agitation. Object constancy is a term
Devised to indicate what a child requires
From days. Clean sheets are an example
Of something that, under many circumstances,
A person can control. The patterns moonlight makes
Are chancier, and dreams, well, dreams
Will have their way with you, their way
With you, will have their way.

LOUISE GLÜCK
(1943–)

Vespers

In your extended absence, you permit me
use of earth, anticipating
some return on investment. I must report
failure in my assignment, principally
regarding the tomato plants.
I think I should not be encouraged to grow
tomatoes. Or, if I am, you should withhold
the heavy rains, the cold nights that come
so often here, while other regions get
twelve weeks of summer. All this
belongs to you: on the other hand,
I planted the seeds, I watched the first shoots
like wings tearing the soil, and it was my heart
broken by the blight, the black spot so quickly
multiplying in the rows. I doubt
you have a heart, in our understanding of
that term. You who do not discriminate
between the dead and the living, who are, in consequence,
immune to foreshadowing, you may not know
how much terror we bear, the spotted leaf,
the red leaves of the maple falling
even in August, in early darkness: I am responsible
for these vines.

ROBERTA HILL
(1947–)

Depot in Rapid City

When the last bus leaves, moths stream toward the lights
like litter in wind. One by one, bulbs dim. The ticket man
locks up, talks of ancestors pale from dreaming.
In this corner, sleep is ugly, the moon vigilant.
Here, hatred taps along sidewalks. He dreams
of wild buses and the one percent he cannot see. You look
down corridors, where building edges whirr at the night,
to find an aged Indian gnawing glass.
Businessmen rub the medicine stones, and wear
crisp smiles that wrinkle in daylight. Muffled,
the heartbeat continues, abandoned stars haunt
the reservations. Clear as tracks,
are callings and cold signals on the wind.

DENISE LEVERTOV
(1923–1997)

The Sharks

Well then, the last day the sharks appeared.
Dark fins appear, innocent
as if in fair warning. The sea becomes
sinister, are they everywhere?
I tell you, they break six feet of water.
Isn't it the same sea, and won't we
play in it any more?
I like it clear and not
too calm, enough waves
to fly in on. For the first time
I dared to swim out of my depth.
It was sundown when they came, the time
when a sheen of copper stills the sea,
not dark enough for moonlight, clear enough
to see them easily. Dark
the sharp lift of the fins.

LORINE NIEDECKER
(1903–1970)

When Ecstasy is Inconvenient

Feign a great calm;
all gay transport soon ends.
Chant: who knows—
flight's end or flight's beginning
for the resting gull?

Heart, be still.
Say there is money but it rusted;
say the time of moon is not right for escape.
It's the color in the lower sky
too broadly suffused,
or the wind in my tie.

Know amazedly how
often one takes his madness
into his own hands
and keeps it.

CHARLIE SMITH
(1947–)

Crostatas

in rome I got down among the weeds and tiny perfumed
flowers like eyeballs dabbed in blood and the big ruins
said *do it my way pal* while starlings
kept offering show biz solutions and well the vatican
pursued its interests the palm trees like singular affidavits
the wind succinct and the mountains painted blue
just before dawn accelerated at the last point
of departure before the big illuminated structures
dug up from the basement got going and I ate crostatas
for breakfast and on the terrace chatted
with the clay-faced old man next door and said I was
after a woman who'd left me years ago and he said lord aren't we all.

ROBINSON JEFFERS
(1887–1962)

To Helen About Her Hair

Your hair is long and wonderful;
It is dark, with golden
Lights in the length of it.

Long, lovely, liquid, glorious,
Is your hair, and lustrous,
Scented with summertime.

Beware when you are combing it,
In the nights and mornings,
Shaking its splendor out.

I bid you comb it carefully,
For my soul is caught there,
Wound in the web of it.

JOHN ASHBERY
(1927–)

Honestly,

we could send you out there
to join the cackle squad,
but hey, that highly accomplished,
thinly regarded equestrian—well there was no way
he was going to join the others' field trip.
Wouldn't put his head on the table.
But here's the thing:

They had owned great dread,
knew of a way to get away from here
through ice and smoke
always clutching her fingers, like it says
to do.

Once we were passionate about the police,
yawned in the teeth of pixels,
but a far rumor blanked us out.
We bathed in moonshine.
Now, experts disagree.
Were we unhappy or sublime?
We'll have to wait until the next time
an angel comes rapping at the door
to rejoice docently.

(I know there's a way to do this.)

JOHN HOLLANDER
(1929–2013)

Late August on the Lido

To lie on these beaches for another summer
Would not become them at all,
And yet the water and her sands will suffer
When, in the fall,
These golden children will be taken from her.

It is not the gold they bring: enough of that
Has shone in the water for ages
And in the bright theater of Venice at their backs;
But the final stages
Of all those afternoons when they played and sat

And waited for a beckoning wind to blow them
Back over the water again
Are scenes most necessary to this ocean.
What actors then
Will play when these disperse from the sand below them?

All this is over until, perhaps, next spring;
This last afternoon must be pleasing.
Europe, Europe is over, but they lie here still,
While the wind, increasing,
Sands teeth, sands eyes, sands taste, sands everything.

H. D.
(1886–1961)

The Wind Sleepers

Whiter
than the crust
left by the tide,
we are stung by the hurled sand
and the broken shells.

We no longer sleep
in the wind—
we awoke and fled
through the city gate.

Tear—
tear us an altar,
tug at the cliff-boulders,
pile them with the rough stones—
we no longer
sleep in the wind,
propitiate us.

Chant in a wail
that never halts,
pace a circle and pay tribute
with a song.

When the roar of a dropped wave
breaks into it,
pour meted words
of sea-hawks and gulls
and sea-birds that cry
discords.

from Monna Innominata

"O ombre vane, fuor che ne l'aspetto!" — Dante
"Immaginata guida la conduce." — Petrarca

I dream of you to wake: would that I might
    Dream of you and not wake but slumber on;
      Nor find with dreams the dear companion gone,
As Summer ended Summer birds take flight.
In happy dreams I hold you full in sight
    I blush again who waking look so wan;
      Brighter than sunniest day that ever shone,
In happy dreams your smile makes day of night.
Thus only in a dream we are at one,
    Thus only in a dream we give and take
      The faith that maketh rich who take or give;
If thus to sleep is sweeter than to wake,
    To die were surely sweeter than to live,
Tho' there be nothing new beneath the sun.

September

The Hand

The teacher asks a question.
You know the answer, you suspect
you are the only one in the classroom
who knows the answer, because the person
in question is yourself, and on that
you are the greatest living authority,
but you don't raise your hand.
You raise the top of your desk
and take out an apple.
You look out the window.
You don't raise your hand and there is
some essential beauty in your fingers,
which aren't even drumming, but lie
flat and peaceful.
The teacher repeats the question.
Outside the window, on an overhanging branch,
a robin is ruffling its feathers
and spring is in the air.

JAMES ARMSTRONG
(1957–)

September

I miss the tilt and racket of your face,
the collapsing factories of your anger,
the shoreline wearing your boas of foam—
the steel mirror of your silence,
your glass contingencies, in the night's hold.
I miss the morning's coverlet of cloud,
one gull flying east over the moving distances
while closer in
the same boulder is kissed again and again.
As the blacksmith plunges the bruised steel into the tub,
erasing the heat of his industry,
I have cooled my brow
with the ice of your disdain—
I have held your cold hand in the rain.

Books

How you loved to read in the snow and when your
face turned to water from the internal heat
combined with the heavy crystals or maybe it was
reversus you went half-blind and your eyelashes
turned to ice the time you walked through swirls
with dirty tears not far from the rat-filled river
or really a mile away—or two—in what
you came to call the Aristotle room
in a small hole outside the Carnegie library.

EILEEN MYLES
(1949–)

Leo Said

you've gotta
write clearer
so you can
be read
when you're
dead

JAMES GALVIN
(1951–)

Post-Modernism

A pinup of Rita Hayworth was taped
To the bomb that fell on Hiroshima.
The avant-garde makes me weep with boredom.
Horses *are* wishes, especially dark ones.

That's why twitches and fences.
That's why switches and spurs.
That's why the idiom of betrayal.
They forgive us.

Their windswayed manes and tails,
Their eyes,
Affront the winterscrubbed prairie
With gentleness.

They live in both worlds and forgive us.
I'll give you a hint: the wind in fits and starts.
Like schoolchildren when the teacher walks in,
The aspens jostle for their places

And fall still.
A delirium of ridges breaks in a blue streak:
A confusion of means
Saved from annihilation

By catastrophe.
A horse gallops up to the gate and stops.
The rider dismounts.
Do I know him?

JAMES TATE
(1943–2015)

The List of Famous Hats

Napoleon's hat is an obvious choice I guess to list as a famous hat, but that's not the hat I have in mind. That was his hat for show. I am thinking of his private bathing cap, which in all honesty wasn't much different than the one any jerk might buy at a corner drugstore now, except for two minor eccentricities. The first one isn't even funny: Simply it was a white rubber bathing cap, but too small. Napoleon led such a hectic life ever since his childhood, even farther back than that, that he never had a chance to buy a new bathing cap and still as a grown-up—well, he didn't really grow that much, but his head did: He was a pinhead at birth, and he used, until his death really, the same little tiny bathing cap that he was born in, and this meant that later it was very painful to him and gave him many headaches, as if he needed more. So, he had to vaseline his skull like crazy to even get the thing on. The second eccentricity was that it was a *tricorn* bathing cap. Scholars like to make a lot out of this, and it would be easy to do. My theory is simple-minded to be sure: that beneath his public head there was another head and it was a pyramid or something.

AMY LOWELL
(1874–1925)

Fragment

What is poetry? Is it a mosaic
   Of coloured stones which curiously are wrought
   Into a pattern? Rather glass that's taught
By patient labor any hue to take
And glowing with a sumptuous splendor, make
   Beauty a thing of awe; where sunbeams caught,
   Transmuted fall in sheafs of rainbows fraught
With storied meaning for religion's sake.

MARILYN NELSON
(1946–)

Daughters, 1900

Five daughters, in the slant light on the porch,
are bickering. The eldest has come home
with new truths she can hardly wait to teach.

She lectures them: the younger daughters search
the sky, elbow each others' ribs, and groan.
Five daughters, in the slant light on the porch

and blue-sprigged dresses, like a stand of birch
saplings whose leaves are going yellow-brown
with new truths. They can hardly wait to teach,

themselves, to be called "Ma'am," to march
high-heeled across the hanging bridge to town.
Five daughters. In the slant light on the porch

Pomp lowers his paper for a while, to watch
the beauties he's begotten with his Ann:
these new truths they can hardly wait to teach.

The eldest sniffs, "A lady doesn't scratch."
The third snorts back, "Knock, knock: nobody home."
The fourth concedes, "Well, maybe not in *church* . . ."
Five daughters in the slant light on the porch.

TED KOOSER
(1939–)

Porch Swing in September

The porch swing hangs fixed in a morning sun
that bleaches its gray slats, its flowered cushion
whose flowers have faded, like those of summer,
and a small brown spider has hung out her web
on a line between porch post and chain
so that no one may swing without breaking it.
She is saying it's time that the swinging were done with,
time that the creaking and pinging and popping
that sang through the ceiling were past,
time now for the soft vibrations of moths,
the wasp tapping each board for an entrance,
the cool dewdrops to brush from her work
every morning, one world at a time.

CAMILLE T. DUNGY
(1972–)

Language

Silence is one part of speech, the war cry
of wind down a mountain pass another.
A stranger's voice echoing through lonely
valleys, a lover's voice rising so close
it's your own tongue: these are keys to cipher,
the way the high hawk's key unlocks the throat
of the sky and the coyote's yip knocks
it shut, the way the aspens' bells conform
to the breeze while the rapid's drums define
resistance. Sage speaks with one voice, pinyon
with another. Rock, wind her hand, water
her brush, spells and then scatters her demands.
Some notes tear and pebble our paths. Some notes
gather: the bank we map our lives around.

MICHAEL PALMER
(1942–)

Dearest Reader

He painted the mountain over and over again
from his place in the cave, agape
at the light, its absence, the mantled
skull with blue-tinted hollows, wren-
like bird plucking berries from the fire
her hair alight and so on
lemon grass in cafe in clear glass.
Dearest reader there were trees
formed of wire, broad entryways
beneath balconies beneath spires
youthful head come to rest in meadow
beside bend in gravel road, still
body of milky liquid
her hair alight and so on
successive halls, flowered carpets and doors
or the photograph of nothing but pigeons
and grackles by the shadow of a fountain.

ALFRED KREYMBORG
(1883–1966)

Poetry

Ladislaw the critic
is five feet six inches high,
which means
that his eyes
are five feet two inches
from the ground,
which means,
if you read him your poem,
and his eyes lift to five feet
and a trifle more than two inches,
what you have done
is Poetry—
should his eyes remain
at five feet two inches,
you have perpetrated prose,
and do his eyes stoop
—which heaven forbid!—
the least trifle below
five feet two inches,
you
are an unspeakable adjective.

LORNA DEE CERVANTES
(1954–)

Multiplication

Four plus zero is a corner in New York
where Lucky plays a pinball sax for change.
One plus one can change your life.
Two times two can grow a family
out of home. Three times six
is a crowded classroom in Jersey
where Maria doesn't have her homework and
Aaron swears too many times one.
Five times five is a banquet on the Upper
East Side where six time six many pigeons
are poisoned into the slams of traffic.
Seven times seven is the number of junkies
nodding. Eight minus seven is the
rhythm of the wait.

ROBERT PINSKY
(1940–)

Improvisation on Yiddish

I've got you in my pocket, Ich hob mir fer pacht.
It sees me and I cannot spell it.

Ich hob dich in bud, which means I see you as if
You were in the bathtub naked: I know you completely.

Kischkas: guts. Tongue of the guts, tongue
Of the heart naked, the guts of the tongue.

Bubbeh loschen. Tongue of my grandmother
That I can't spell in these characters I know.

I know "Hob dich in bud" which means I see you
And through you, tongue of irony. Intimate.

Tongue of the dear and the dead, tongue of death.
Tongue of laughing in the guts, naked and completely.

Bubbeh loschen, lost tongue of the lost, "Get away
From me" which means, *come closer*: Gei

Avek fun mir, Ich hob dich in bud. I see you
Completely. Naked. I've got you in my pocket.

HYAM PLUTZIK
(1911–1962)

On Hearing That My Poems Were Being Studied in a Distant Place

What are they mumbling about me there?
"Here," they say, "he suffered; here was glad."
Are words clothes or the putting off of clothes?

The scene is as follows: my book is open
On thirty desks; the teacher expounds my life.
Outside the window the Pacific roars like a lion.

Beside which my small words rise and fall.
"In this alliteration a tower crashed."
Are words clothes or the putting off of clothes?

"Here, in the fisherman casting on the water,
He saw the end of the dreamer.
And in that image, death, naked."

Out of my life I fashioned a fistful of words.
When I opened my hand, they flew away.

THOMAS HARDY
(1840–1928)

The High-School Lawn

Gray prinked with rose,
White tipped with blue,
Shoes with gay hose,
Sleeves of chrome hue;
Fluffed frills of white,
Dark bordered light;
Such shimmerings through
Trees of emerald green are eyed
This afternoon, from the road outside.

They whirl around:
Many laughters run
With a cascade's sound;
Then a mere one.

A bell: they flee:
Silence then:—
So it will be
Some day again
With them,—with me.

NICK FLYNN
(1960–)

Forty-Seven Minutes

I ask a high school class to locate an image in a poem we've just read—
their heads at this moment are bowed to the page. After some back &
forth about the rain & a styrofoam cup, a girl raises her hand & asks,
Does it matter? I smile—it's as if the universe was balanced on those three
words & we've landed in the unanswerable & I have to admit that no, it
doesn't, not really, matter, if rain is an image or rain is an idea or rain is
a sound in our heads. *But to get through the next forty-seven minutes we
might have to pretend it does.*

JOSEPH FASANO
(1982–   )

Late Processional

Slowly I am learning to give
the names of things their solitude.
When I go to myself, I find
my throat flushed with a chorus

of black wings. Was this the earth
hunting out its given name
or another blind thing
brought down?

ANGELINA WELD GRIMKÉ
(1880–1958)

El Beso

Twilight—and you,
Quiet—the stars;
Snare of the shine of your teeth,
Your provocative laughter,
The gloom of your hair;
Lure of you, eye and lip,
Yearning, yearning,
Languor, surrender;
    Your mouth
And madness, madness
Tremulous, breathless, flaming,
The space of a sigh;
Then awaking—remembrance,
Pain, regret—your sobbing;
And again quiet—the stars,
Twilight—and you.

CAROLYN FORCHÉ
(1950–)

Sequestered Writing

Horses were turned loose in the child's sorrow. Black and roan, cantering
   through snow.
The way light fills the hand with light, November with graves, infancy
   with white.
White. Given lilacs, lilacs disappear. Then low voices rising in walls.
The way they withdrew from the child's body and spoke as if it were not
   there.

What ghost comes to the bedside whispering *You*?
—With its *no one* without its *I*—
A dwarf ghost? A closet of empty clothes?
Ours was a ghost who stole household goods. Nothing anyone would
   miss.
Supper plates. Apples. Barbed wire behind the house.

At the end of the hall, it sleepwalks into a mirror wearing mother's robe.
A bedsheet lifts from the bed and hovers. Face with no face. *Come here*.
The bookcase knows, and also the darkness of books. Long passages *into*,
Endless histories *toward*, sleeping pages *about*. Why else toss gloves into
   a grave?

A language that once sent ravens through firs. The open world from
   which it came.
Words holding the scent of an asylum fifty years. It is fifty years, then.
The child hears from within: *Come here and know*, below

And unbeknownst to us, what these fields had been.

MATT RASMUSSEN
(1975–)

Skyscraper

A sword thrust
into the city.

From inside
the café, the letters

on the window
look like a new

language. It's this
simple: There is

nothing within us
like what we are

inside this window.
Colossal seppuku,

you are the sky
before the sky.

BOB HICOK
(1960–   )

In Michael Robins's
class minus one

At the desk where the boy sat, he sees the Chicago River.
It raises its hand.
It asks if metaphor should burn.
He says fire is the basis for all forms of the mouth.
He asks, why did you fill the boy with your going?
I didn't know a boy had been added to me, the river says.
Would you have given him back if you knew?
I think so, the river says, I have so many boys in me,
            I'm worn out stroking eyes looking up at the day.
Have you written a poem for us? he asks the river,
            and the river reads its poem,
            and the other students tell the river
            it sounds like a poem the boy would have written,
            that they smell the boy's cigarettes
            in the poem, they feel his teeth
            biting the page.
And the river asks, did this boy dream of horses?
            because I suddenly dream of horses, I suddenly dream.
They're in a circle and the river says, I've never understood
            round things, why would leaving come back
            to itself?
And a girl makes a kiss with her mouth and leans it
            against the river, and the kiss flows away
            but the river wants it back, the river makes sounds
            to go after the kiss.
And they all make sounds for the river to carry to the boy.
And the river promises to never surrender the boy's shape
            to the ocean.

WILLIAM CARLOS WILLIAMS
(1883–1963)

Willow Poem

It is a willow when summer is over,
a willow by the river
from which no leaf has fallen nor
bitten by the sun
turned orange or crimson.
The leaves cling and grow paler,
swing and grow paler
over the swirling waters of the river
as if loath to let go,
they are so cool, so drunk with
the swirl of the wind and of the river—
oblivious to winter,
the last to let go and fall
into the water and on the ground.

NOAH FALCK
(1977–)

Poem Excluding Fiction

We live in the most fortunate of times. And
who's to blame? Our moods like the four
seasons in a tinted window overlooking a
bank robbery. Everyone is raising children
on cable television, on leashes, on the slot
machines that have become our elegies. We
live other lives in high school, college, on the
porch reading the obituaries. Say I miss you
into the mirror while shaving, brushing teeth,
plucking something meant to grow forever.

THOMAS LUX
(1946–)

You and Your Ilk

I have thought much upon
who might be my ilk,
and that I am ilk myself if I have ilk.
Is one of my ilk, or me, the barber
who cuts the hair of the blind?
And the man crushed by cruelties
for which we can't imagine sorrow,
who would be his ilk?
And whose ilk was it
standing around, hands in pockets, May 1933,
when 2,242 tons of books were burned?
So, what makes my ilkness *my*
ilkness? No answers, none obtainable.
To be one of the ilks, that's all
I hoped for; to say hello to the mailman,
nod to my neighbors, watch
my children climb the stairs of a big yellow bus
that takes them to a place
where they learn to read
and write and eat their lunches
from puzzle trays—all around them, amid
the clatter and din,
amid bananas, bread, and milk.
all around them: them and *their* ilk.

ALLISON BENIS WHITE
(1972–)

from Please Bury Me in This

Maybe my arms lifted as a woman lowers a dress over my head.

This is not what I want to tell you.

Looking at red flowers on her mother's dress as she sat on her lap on a train is Woolf's first memory.

Then the sound of waves behind a yellow shade, of being alive as ecstasy.

Maybe her mind, as I read, lowering over my mind.

Maybe looking down, as I sit on the floor, at the book inside the diamond of my legs.

Even briefly, to love with someone else's mind.

Moving my lips as I read *the waves breaking, one, two, one, two, and sending a splash of water over the beach.*

What I want to tell you is ecstasy.

JENNIFER CHANG
(1976-   )

End Note

Before words, there was the language of the mark.
We moved a stick along the dirt and drew
a line to the end. Our wild flickers
ink-streaked a page, symbols like the stars'
orphaned radiance giving more light
than reason. He holds out a hand: *What do you see?*
Skin of absolution, there is nothing. I wrote S
before I learned the letter; and when he warned
Be silent as the "e" in house, I woke our father.
He had outgrown me with his name.
More wisp than dart, the sun rarely finds us
in the forest: he holds the fruit—I see
a breath vanishing—he knows the spell:
I live for a word, wordlessly.

CHARLES SIMIC
(1938–)

Late September

The mail truck goes down the coast
Carrying a single letter.
At the end of a long pier
The bored seagull lifts a leg now and then
And forgets to put it down.
There is a menace in the air
Of tragedies in the making.

Last night you thought you heard television
In the house next door.
You were sure it was some new
Horror they were reporting,
So you went out to find out.
Barefoot, wearing just shorts.
It was only the sea sounding weary
After so many lifetimes
Of pretending to be rushing off somewhere
And never getting anywhere.

This morning, it felt like Sunday.
The heavens did their part
By casting no shadow along the boardwalk
Or the row of vacant cottages,
Among them a small church
With a dozen gray tombstones huddled close
As if they, too, had the shivers.

LEIGH STEIN
(1984–)

The Dream of a
Common Language

after Adrienne Rich

On Wednesdays I take the train past Yankee Stadium,
to a place where it is never a given that I speak the language,
to a place where graffiti covers the mural they painted to hide
the graffiti, to a place where the children call me *Miss Miss*
Miss Miss Miss and I find in one of their poems, a self-portrait,
the line *I wish I was rish*. The dream of a common language

is the language of one million dollars, of basketball, of plátanos.
Are the kids black? my boyfriend wants to know. Dominican.
It's different. When asked to write down a question
they wish they could ask their mom or dad, one boy writes,
Paper or plastic? A girl in the back of the class wants to know
Why don't I have lycene, translating the sound of the color

of my skin into her own language. The best poet
in sixth grade is the girl who is this year repeating
sixth grade. When I tell her teacher of her talent
she says, *At least now we know she's good*
at something. To speak their language, I study
the attendance list, practice the cadence of their names.

Yesterday I presented a black and white portrait of a black man,
his bald head turned away from us, a spotted moth resting
on one shoulder. I told them this is a man serving a life
sentence in Louisiana. Is this art? Without hesitation,

one girl said no, why would anybody
want to take a picture
of that.

NIKKI GIOVANNI
(1943–)

My First Memory (of Librarians)

This is my first memory:
A big room with heavy wooden tables that sat on a creaky wood floor
A line of green shades—bankers' lights—down the center
Heavy oak chairs that were too low or maybe I was simply too short
       For me to sit in and read
So my first book was always big

In the foyer up four steps a semicircular desk presided
To the left side the card catalog
On the right newspapers draped over what looked like a quilt rack
Magazines face out from the wall

The welcoming smile of my librarian
The anticipation in my heart
All those books—another world—just waiting
At my fingertips

October

JAMES WRIGHT
(1927–1980)

Autumn Begins in Martins Ferry, Ohio

In the Shreve High football stadium,
I think of Polacks nursing long beers in Tiltonsville,
And gray faces of Negroes in the blast furnace at Benwood,
And the ruptured night watchman of Wheeling Steel,
Dreaming of heroes.

All the proud fathers are ashamed to go home.
Their women cluck like starved pullets,
Dying for love.

Therefore,
Their sons grow suicidally beautiful
At the beginning of October,
And gallop terribly against each other's bodies.

CARL SANDBURG
(1878–1967)

Autumn Movement

I cried over beautiful things knowing no beautiful thing lasts.

The field of cornflower yellow is a scarf at the neck of the copper sun-
burned woman, the mother of the year, the taker of seeds.

The northwest wind comes and the yellow is torn full of holes, new beau-
tiful things come in the first spit of snow on the northwest wind,
and the old things go, not one lasts.

BRENDA HILLMAN
(1951–)

The Hour Until We See You

When we part, even for an hour,
you become the standing on the avenue
baffled one, under neon,
    holding that huge
red book about the capital—;

    what will you be in the next hour,
  —bundled to walk
through creamy coins from streetlamps
on sidewalks to your car, past
  candles reflected in windows, while
mineral sirens fade in the don't-
return,—driving home past
  pre-spring plum blossom riot
moments of your thought . . .

      Those trees rush to rust leaves,
each a time-hinge with great energy—
they can't bear inexactitude.
News of revolts in the squares—there—
  & here, the envious have gone to cafés
to speak in order to leave things out—
    Love, literature is in flames,
  it was meant to be specific—;
  you have driven past these rooms
ten thousand times to make your report;
make your report;
    you will never forget how you felt—

MARK DOTY
(1953–)

Theory of Beauty (Pompeii)

Tiny girl in line at the café—seven, eight?—holding her book open,
pointing to the words and saying them half-aloud
while her mother attends to ordering breakfast;

she's reading POMPEII . . . Buried Alive! with evident delight.
Pleasure with a little shiver inside it.

And that evening, I thought I was no longer afraid
of the death's head beneath the face of the man beneath me.

LARRY SAWYER
(1970–)

Sundial

for James Wright

The poet will seek to clothe herself in sparrows.

A motor in each leaf
distills autumn's engines and we're off.

Upstart cartoon morning;
    these various roosters scratch inside the eyelids
    and declare beneath the streetlamps that their
    moats are filled with vowels.

That the life alone is not wasted but
rich with a pageantry of else.
Who absconds with our best sense
and seizes us by the throat as we untangle ourselves
from lovers and, draped in fever, split the
night into halves?   Each contains a commercial
advertising just that.

        Despite his tactics, fully rejecting experience
the candid creator winces at the audience's heightened
passing.
    Remain, in secret,

a pea of concern, in some harbor of ghostly direction.
    There lurks an I among those hours.

JENNY BOULLY
(1976–)

not merely because of the unknown
that was stalking toward them
[but the rocking chair]

But the rocking chair appears to be missing *a little something*. If you
hang the birdcage there, we'll hear its singing. Keep the curtains sheer
drawn over the four poster—that's the kind of bed *I would like to have*.
I will can the preserves; I will can the preserves so that come autumn,
come autumn when I have hung up the dustpan, you will have this small
bit of apricot to remember. Me by. I don't think I quite believe in *that*
anymore, and besides, this here tooth has fallen out; it's the last one I've
needed for quite a while. I will cut the slices of apple *for you*; I will shake
the grove of bramble bushes *for you*; the raspberries, too tart, too tart, I
will lemon and sugar them for you, 'cause that is what mother has taught.
My dear, did I write down all of my symptoms this morning? Has the
paper been left right on our doorstep? I do believe, Wendy, I do believe
that Smee has stolen it.

RICHARD WILBUR
(1921–)

The Beautiful Changes

One wading a Fall meadow finds on all sides
The Queen Anne's Lace lying like lilies
On water; it glides
So from the walker, it turns
Dry grass to a lake, as the slightest shade of you
Valleys my mind in fabulous blue Lucernes.

The beautiful changes as a forest is changed
By a chameleon's tuning his skin to it;
As a mantis, arranged
On a green leaf, grows
Into it, makes the leaf leafier, and proves
Any greenness is deeper than anyone knows.

Your hands hold roses always in a way that says
They are not only yours; the beautiful changes
In such kind ways,
Wishing ever to sunder
Things and things' selves for a second finding, to lose
For a moment all that it touches back to wonder.

MINA LOY
(1882–1966)

Moreover, the Moon———

Face of the skies
preside
over our wonder.

Fluorescent
truant of heaven
draw us under.

Silver, circular corpse
your decease
infects us with unendurable ease,

touching nerve-terminals
to thermal icicles

Coercive as coma, frail as bloom
innuendoes of your inverse dawn
suffuse the self;
our every corpuscle become an elf.

EDNA ST. VINCENT MILLAY
(1892–1950)

Ebb

I know what my heart is like
    Since your love died:
It is like a hollow ledge
Holding a little pool
    Left there by the tide,
    A little tepid pool,
Drying inward from the edge.

ROBERT FROST
(1874–1963)

The Oven Bird

There is a singer everyone has heard,
Loud, a mid-summer and a mid-wood bird,
Who makes the solid tree trunks sound again.
He says that leaves are old and that for flowers
Mid-summer is to spring as one to ten.
He says the early petal-fall is past
When pear and cherry bloom went down in showers
On sunny days a moment overcast;
And comes that other fall we name the fall.
He says the highway dust is over all.
The bird would cease and be as other birds
But that he knows in singing not to sing.
The question that he frames in all but words
Is what to make of a diminished thing.

T. E. HULME
(1883–1917)

Autumn

A touch of cold in the Autumn night
I walked abroad,
And saw the ruddy moon lean over a hedge
Like a red-faced farmer.
I did not stop to speak, but nodded;
And round about were the wistful stars
With white faces like town children.

CHRISTIAN WIMAN
(1966–)

Hard Night

What words or harder gift
does the light require of me
carving from the dark
this difficult tree?

What place or farther peace
do I almost see
emerging from the night
and heart of me?

The sky whitens, goes on and on.
Fields wrinkle into rows
of cotton, go on and on.
Night like a fling of crows
disperses and is gone.

What song, what home,
what calm or one clarity
can I not quite come to,
never quite see:
this field, this sky, this tree.

DAVID LEHMAN
(1948–)

Autumn Evening

(after Holderlin)

The yellow pears hang in the lake.
Life sinks, grace reigns, sins ripen, and
in the north dies an almond tree.

A genius took me by the hand and said
come with me though the time has not yet come.

Therefore, when the gods get lonely,
a hero will emerge from the bushes
of a summer evening
bearing the first green figs of the season.

For the glory of the gods has lain asleep
too long in the dark
in darkness too long
too long in the dark.

JOANNA FUHRMAN
(1972–)

Not Here, Exactly

I found your letter
in the pocket

of a borrowed goat.

It showed me
the way—

small as an eye.

One mountain tried
to taste another,

then spit it out.

Your letter called
all the other letters

"friends."

You too were
my friend,

soft as a melting
or melted nail.

Dear little cage,
dark plum.

Affirmation

To grow old is to lose everything.
Aging, everybody knows it.
Even when we are young,
we glimpse it sometimes, and nod our heads
when a grandfather dies.
Then we row for years on the midsummer
pond, ignorant and content. But a marriage,
that began without harm, scatters
into debris on the shore,
and a friend from school drops
cold on a rocky strand.
If a new love carries us
past middle age, our wife will die
at her strongest and most beautiful.
New women come and go. All go.
The pretty lover who announces
that she is temporary
is temporary. The bold woman,
middle-aged against our old age,
sinks under an anxiety she cannot withstand.
Another friend of decades estranges himself
in words that pollute thirty years.
Let us stifle under mud at the pond's edge
and affirm that it is fitting
and delicious to lose everything.

LUCIE BROCK-BROIDO
(1956–)

Dove, Interrupted

Don't do that when you are dead like this, I said,
Arguably still squabbling about the word inarguably.
I haunt Versailles, poring through the markets of the medieval.
Mostly meat to be sold there; mutton hangs
Like laundry pinkened on its line.
       And gold!—a chalice with a cure for living in it.
We step over the skirt of an Elizabeth.
Red grapes, a delicacy, each peeled for us—
The vestments of a miniature priest, disrobed.
A sister is an old world sparrow placed in a satin shoe.
The weakling's saddle is worn down from just too much sad attitude.
No one wants to face the "opaque reality" of herself.
                     For the life of me.
I was made American. You must consider this.
Whatever suffering is insufferable is punishable by perishable.
In Vienne, the rabbit Maurice is at home in the family cage.
I ache for him, his boredom and his solitude.
On suffering and animals, inarguably, they do.
                I miss your heart, my heart.

AMY LOWELL
(1874–1925)

Autumn

They brought me a quilled, yellow dahlia,
Opulent, flaunting.
Round gold
Flung out of a pale green stalk.
Round, ripe gold
Of maturity,
Meticulously frilled and flaming,
A fire-ball of proclamation:
Fecundity decked in staring yellow
For all the world to see.
They brought a quilled, yellow dahlia,
To me who am barren.
Shall I send it to you,
You who have taken with you
All I once possessed?

CLAUDE MCKAY
(1889–1943)

I Know My Soul

I plucked my soul out of its secret place,
And held it to the mirror of my eye,
To see it like a star against the sky,
A twitching body quivering in space,
A spark of passion shining on my face.
And I explored it to determine why
This awful key to my infinity
Conspires to rob me of sweet joy and grace.
And if the sign may not be fully read,
If I can comprehend but not control,
I need not gloom my days with futile dread,
Because I see a part and not the whole.
Contemplating the strange, I'm comforted
By this narcotic thought: I know my soul.

ERIC PANKEY
(1959–)

Epitaph

Beyond the traceries of the auroras,
The fires of tattered sea foam,
The ghost-terrain of submerged icebergs;
Beyond a cinder dome's black sands;
Beyond peninsula and archipelago,
Archipelago and far-flung islands,
You have made of exile a homeland,
Voyager, and of that chosen depth, a repose.

The eel shimmers and the dogfish darts,
A dance of crisscrosses and trespasses
Through distillate glints and nacreous silts,
And the sun, like fronds of royal palm
Wind-torn, tossed, lashes upon the wake,
But no lamplight mars or bleaches your realm,
A dark of sediment, spawn, slough, and lees,
Runoff, pitch-black, from the rivers of Psalms.

LYN HEJINIAN
(1941–)

Unfollowed Figment

Useless lighthouse, and the bucket on the beach, the tattered begonia
Forget examples—there's not an entity or detail around that isn't more
than a mere example
What's truly funny?
Once upon a time there was a mouse, and there was a cactus and a pair of
very small rubber
    boots with a hole in the sole of the left one, and now that I think back I
remember that there
    was a baby on a barge in a lake full of flowers, and out of these there's a
story to weave
    and probably more than one
The music changes at the mantel, the bassoonist is baffled, the
synchronizer fails
Rickety marble, wet wood, the road narrowing into the distance and then
turning around a rock
Is it empty good writing, is it research, resurgence, repartee?
8, 9, 10, 11, minus 31, 8
A stranger creates an occasion
Lewd silver sea, your bigness carries barges as noon stands in grass
See, I got cops—or they got me; so says the melancholy memoirist from
the anarchy of her
    dreams
Clear is the sojourn
In the stiff air, down the unbalanced wind, over dusty culverts, women
bear their hot cells of
    benevolence
Are all wonders small?

MARY JO BANG
(1946–)

Catastrophe Theory III

Now we sit and play with a tiny toy
elephant that travels a taut string.
Now we are used and use in turn
each other. Our hats unravel
and that in itself is tragic.
To be lost. To have lost. Verbs

like veritable engines pulling the train
of thought forward. The hat is over-
turned and out comes a rabbit. Out comes a man
with a monocle. Out comes a Kaiser.
Yikes, it's history, that ceiling
comprised of recessed squares, each leg a lifeline,

each lie a wife's leg. A pulled velvet cord
rings a bell and everyone comes running
to watch while a year plummets
into the countdown of an open mouth. A loop of razor wire
closes around the circumference of a shaken globe
of snow. Yellowed newsprint with its watery text,

a latticework of shadow thrown
onto the clear screen of the prison wall.
From a mere idea comes the twine
that gives totality its name. What is a theory
but a tentacle reaching for a wafer of reason.
The inevitable gap tragic. Sure, tragic.

CALE YOUNG RICE
(1872–1943)

Haunted Seas

A gleaming glassy ocean,
  Under a sky of gray;
A tide that dreams of motion,
  Or moves, as the dead may;
A bird that dips and wavers
  O'er the lone waters round,
Then with a cry that quavers
  Is gone — a spectral sound.

The brown sad sea-weed drifting
  Far from the land, and lost.
The faint warm fog unlifting,
  The derelict long-tossed,
But now at rest — tho haunted
  By the death-scenting shark,
Whose prey no more undaunted
  Slips from it, spent and stark.

RAE ARMANTROUT
(1947–)

Unbidden

The ghosts swarm.
They speak as one
person. Each
loves you. Each
has left something
undone.

•

Did the palo verde
blush yellow
all at once?

Today's edges
are so sharp

they might cut
anything that moved.

•

The way a lost
word

will come back
unbidden.

You're not interested
in it now,

only
in knowing
where it's been.

CHRISTINA ROSSETTI
(1830–1894)

Song

When I am dead, my dearest,
   Sing no sad songs for me;
Plant thou no roses at my head,
   Nor shady cypress tree:
Be the green grass above me
   With showers and dewdrops wet:
And if thou wilt, remember,
   And if thou wilt, forget.

I shall not see the shadows,
   I shall not feel the rain;
I shall not hear the nightingale
   Sing on as if in pain:
And dreaming through the twilight
   That doth not rise nor set,
Haply I may remember,
   And haply may forget.

from Sharking of the Birdcage

what was it you
wanted us to
say after you died
it's awful without you making sound exist
you said *ponder* this
but none of us can remember
what now dear please speak up
when quaking became zeal to open
nothing now but a
medieval barking gargoyle
whoever gave you the tambourine shall
be sheriff of my tender zoo
I am not here
I am in the future
where I have always been
please hurry back and forth to
kiss me my ghost

DANA LEVIN
(1965–)

Ghosts That Need Reminding

Through shattered glass and sheeted furniture, chicken
wire and piled dishes, sheared-off doors stacked five to a
wall, you're walking like cripples. Toward a dirty window,
obstructed by stacks of chairs.

And once you move them, one by one, palm circles through
the grime and cup your hands round your faces, finally able
to see through—

Charged night. Sheet-flashes of green, threaded with sparks,
the pale orange pan of the moon—

Finally, what turns the wheel: the moon ghosting a hole
through a rainbow, the rainbow's rage to efface the moon,
which the moon sails through slow as a ship, in the shape of a
cross-legged Buddha . . .

Lotus-folded, a figurine. The kind you once found in the
Chinatown markets, for a dollar and a dime—

Saying, You're dying, you're dead. You can withdraw from this
orbit of mirrors.

JACK SPICER
(1925–1965)

Orfeo

Sharp as an arrow Orpheus
Points his music downward.
Hell is there
At the bottom of the seacliff.
Heal
Nothing by this music.
Eurydice
Is a frigate bird or a rock or some seaweed.
Hail nothing
The infernal
Is a slippering wetness out at the horizon.
Hell is this:
The lack of anything but the eternal to look at
The expansiveness of salt
The lack of any bed but one's
Music to sleep in.

CYNTHIA CRUZ
(1968–)

Guidebooks for the Dead

Mother's crimson leather bags
Crammed with saint cards
And tiny glass bottles of liquor.

The bright stitch
Of God's final coming.

Dirt and dregs, silt and stars.

The sweet song
Of poverty

Rinsing through me
Like the memory
Of a dream.

CHRISTOPHER KENNEDY
(1955–)

Ghost in the Land of Skeletons

for Russell Edson

If not for flesh's pretty paint, we're just a bunch of skeletons, working
hard to deny the fact of bones. Teeth remind me that we die. That's why
I never smile, except when looking at a picture of a ghost, captured by
a camera lens, in a book about the paranormal. When someone takes
a picture of a spirit, it gives me hope. I admire the ones who refuse to
go away. Lovers scorned and criminals burned. I love the dead little girl
who plays in her yard, a spectral game of hide and seek. It's the fact they
don't know they're dead that appeals to me most. Like a man once said to
me, *Do you ever feel like you're a ghost? Sure,* I answered, *every day.* He
laughed at that and disappeared. All I could think was he beat me to it.

JOHN BERRYMAN
(1914–1972)

Dream Song 29

There sat down, once, a thing on Henry's heart
só heavy, if he had a hundred years
& more, & weeping, sleepless, in all them time
Henry could not make good.
Starts again always in Henry's ears
the little cough somewhere, an odour, a chime.

And there is another thing he has in mind
like a grave Sienese face a thousand years
would fail to blur the still profiled reproach of. Ghastly,
with open eyes, he attends, blind.
All the bells say: too late. This is not for tears;
thinking.

But never did Henry, as he thought he did,
end anyone and hacks her body up
and hide the pieces, where they may be found.
He knows: he went over everyone, & nobody's missing.
Often he reckons, in the dawn, them up.
Nobody is ever missing.

Ever

Never, never, never, never, never.
—King Lear

Even now I can't grasp "nothing" or "never."
They're unholdable, unglobable, no map to nothing.
Never? Never ever again to see you?
An error, I aver. You're never nothing,
because nothing's not a thing.
I know death is absolute, forever,
the guillotine—gutting—never to which we never say goodbye.
But even as I think "forever" it goes "ever"
and "ever" and "ever." Ever after.
I'm a thing that keeps on thinking. So I never see you
is not a thing or think my mouth can ever. Aver:
You're not "nothing." But neither are you something.
Will I ever really get never?
You're gone. Nothing, never—ever.

November

WALLACE STEVENS
(1879–1955)

Final Soliloquy of
the Interior Paramour

Light the first light of evening, as in a room
In which we rest and, for small reason, think
The world imagined is the ultimate good.

This is, therefore, the intensest rendezvous.
It is in that thought that we collect ourselves,
Out of all the indifferences, into one thing:

Within a single thing, a single shawl
Wrapped tightly round us, since we are poor, a warmth,
A light, a power, the miraculous influence.

Here, now, we forget each other and ourselves.
We feel the obscurity of an order, a whole,
A knowledge, that which arranged the rendezvous.

Within its vital boundary, in the mind.
We say God and the imagination are one . . .
How high that highest candle lights the dark.

Out of this same light, out of the central mind,
We make a dwelling in the evening air,
In which being there together is enough.

BRUCE WEIGL
(1949–)

Home

I didn't know I was grateful
            for such late-autumn
                        bent-up cornfields

yellow in the after-harvest
            sun before the
                        cold plow turns it all over

into never.
            I didn't know
                        I would enter this music

that translates the world
            back into dirt fields
                        that have always called to me

as if I were a thing
            come from the dirt,
                        like a tuber,

or like a needful boy. End
            lonely days, I believe. End the exiled
                        and unraveling strangeness.

Wine Tasting

I think I detect cracked leather.
I'm pretty sure I smell the cherries
from a Shirley Temple my father bought me

in 1959, in a bar in Orlando, Florida,
and the chlorine from my mother's bathing cap.
And last winter's kisses, like salt on black ice,

like the moon slung away from the earth.
When Li Po drank wine, the moon dove
in the river, and he staggered after.

Probably he tasted laughter.
When my friend Susan drinks
she cries because she's Irish

and childless. I'd like to taste,
one more time, the rain that arrived
one afternoon and fell just short

of where I stood, so I leaned my face in,
alive in both worlds at once,
knowing it would end and not caring.

DONALD REVELL
(1954–)

Election Year

A jet of mere phantom
Is a brook, as the land around
Turns rocky and hollow.
Those airplane sounds
Are the drowning of bicyclists.
Leaping, a bridesmaid leaps.
You asked for my autobiography.
Imagine the greeny clicking sound
Of hummingbirds in a dry wood,
And there you'd have it. Other birds
Pour over the walls now.
I'd never suspected: every day,
Although the nation is done for,
I find new flowers.

ADELAIDE CRAPSEY
(1878–1914)

November Night

Listen . . .
With faint dry sound,
Like steps of passing ghosts,
The leaves, frost-crisp'd, break from the trees
And fall.

AFAA MICHAEL WEAVER
(1951–)

Flux

I am a city of bones
deep inside my marrow,
a song in electric chords,
decrescendo to mute, rise
to white noise, half silences
in a blank harmony as all
comes to nothing, my eyes
the central fire of my soul,
yellow, orange, red—gone
in an instant and then back
when I am, for a glimpse,
as precise as a bird's breath,
when I am perfect, undone
by hope when hope will not
listen, the moon wasting
to where I need not worry
that bones turn to ash,
a brittle staccato in dust.

ELLEN BASS
(1947–)

Eating the Bones

The women in my family
strip the succulent
flesh from broiled chicken,
scrape the drumstick clean;
bite off the cartilage, chew the gristle,
crush the porous swellings
at the ends of each slender baton.
With strong molars
they split the tibia, sucking out
the dense marrow.
They use up love, they swallow
every dark grain,
so at the end there's nothing left,
a scant pile of splinters
on the empty white plate.

JOSHUA BECKMAN
(1971–)

In Colorado, in Oregon, upon

In Colorado, in Oregon, upon
each beloved fork, a birthday is celebrated.
I miss each and every one of my friends.
I believe in getting something for nothing.
Push the chair, and what I can tell you
with almost complete certainty
is that the chair won't mind.
And beyond hope,
I expect it is like this everywhere.
Music soothing people.
Change rolling under tables.
The immaculate cutoff so that we may continue.
A particular pair of trees waking up against the window.
This partnership of mind, and always now
in want of forgiveness. That forgiveness be
the domain of the individual,
like music or personal investment.
Great forward-thinking people brought us
the newspaper, and look what we have done.
It is time for forgiveness. Dear ones,
unmistakable quality will soon be upon us.
Don't wait for anything else.

TODD BOSS
(1968–)

I Love the Hour Just Before

a party. Everybody
at home getting
ready. Pulling
on boots, fixing
their hair, planning
what to say if
she's there, picking
a pluckier lipstick,
rehearsing a joke
with a stickpin
in it, doing
the last minute
fumbling one does
before leaving for
the night like
tying up the dog or
turning on the yard
light. I like to think
of them driving,
finding their way
in the dark, taking
this left, that right,
while I light candles,
start the music softly
seething. Everything
waiting. Even
the wine barely
breathing.

LI-YOUNG LEE
(1957–)

Eating Together

In the steamer is the trout
seasoned with slivers of ginger,
two sprigs of green onion, and sesame oil.
We shall eat it with rice for lunch,
brothers, sister, my mother who will
taste the sweetest meat of the head,
holding it between her fingers
deftly, the way my father did
weeks ago. Then he lay down
to sleep like a snow-covered road
winding through pines older than him,
without any travelers, and lonely for no one.

HELEN HUNT JACKSON
(1830–1885)

November

This is the treacherous month when autumn days
With summer's voice come bearing summer's gifts.
Beguiled, the pale down-trodden aster lifts
Her head and blooms again. The soft, warm haze
Makes moist once more the sere and dusty ways,
And, creeping through where dead leaves lie in drifts,
The violet returns. Snow noiseless sifts
Ere night, an icy shroud, which morning's rays
Will idly shine upon and slowly melt,
Too late to bid the violet live again.
The treachery, at last, too late, is plain;
Bare are the places where the sweet flowers dwelt.
What joy sufficient hath November felt?
What profit from the violet's day of pain?

Around Us

We need some pines to assuage the darkness
when it blankets the mind,
we need a silvery stream that banks as smoothly
as a plane's wing, and a worn bed of
needles to pad the rumble that fills the mind,
and a blur or two of a wild thing
that sees and is not seen. We need these things
between appointments, after work,
and, if we keep them, then someone someday,
lying down after a walk
and supper, with the fire hole wet down,
the whole night sky set at a particular
time, without numbers or hours, will cause
a little sound of thanks—a zipper or a snap—
to close round the moment and the thought
of whatever good we did.

RICHARD SIKEN
(1967–)

Detail of the Hayfield

I followed myself for a long while, deep into the field.
Two heads full of garbage.

Our scope was larger than I realized,
which only made me that much more responsible.

Yellow, yellow, gold, and ocher.
We stopped. We held the field. We stood very still.

Everyone needs a place.

You need it for the moment you need it, then you bless it—
thank you soup, thank you flashlight—

and move on. Who does this? No one.

playing with fire

something is always burning, passion,
> pride, envy, desire, the internal organs
> going chokingly up in smoke, as some-
> > thing outside the body exerts a pull
that drags us like a match across sand-
> > paper. something is always burning,
> london, paris, detroit, l.a., the neighbor-

> > hoods no one outside seems to see until
they're backlit by flames, when the out-
> > siders, peering through dense, acrid,
> black-&-orange-rimmed fumes, mis-
> > take their dark reflections for savages
altogether alien. how hot are the london
> > riots for west end pearls? how hot in tot-

> tenham? if one bead of cream rolls down
one precious neck, heads will roll in brix-
ton: the science of sociology. the mark
> > duggan principle of cause and effect:
> under conditions of sufficient pressure—
> > measured roughly in years + lead ÷ £s—
black blood is highly combustible.

FADY JOUDAH
(1971–)

Names

Thank you for dreaming of me
for letting me know
for waking up to remember that you dreamed
I never wake up when I dream of you

What woke you up
was it someone
else's body?

A small thrill a little secret is ours
a desire for safe travel
in unspilled blood

ROBERT LOUIS STEVENSON
(1850–1894)

My House, I Say (XXXVI)

My house, I say. But hark to the sunny doves
That make my roof the arena of their loves,
That gyre about the gable all day long
And fill the chimneys with their murmurous song:
Our house, they say; and MINE, the cat declares
And spreads his golden fleece upon the chairs;
And *mine* the dog, and rises stiff with wrath
If any alien foot profane the path.
So too the buck that trimmed my terraces,
Our whilome gardener, called the garden his;
Who now, deposed, surveys my plain abode
And his late kingdom, only from the road.

Why They Went

that men might learn what the world is like at the spot where
the sun does not decline in the heavens.
—Apsley Cherry-Garrard

Frost bitten. Snow blind. Hungry. Craving
fresh pie and hot toddies, a whole roasted
unflippered thing to carve. Craving a bed
that had, an hour before entering,
been warmed with a stone from the hearth.

Always back to Eden—to the time when we knew
with certainty that something watched and loved us.
That the very air was miraculous and ours.
That all we had to do was show up.

The sun rolled along the horizon. The light never left them.
The air from their warm mouths became diamonds.
And they longed for everything they did not have.
And they came home and longed again.

MARILYN NELSON
(1946–)

Dusting

Thank you for these tiny
particles of ocean salt,
pearl-necklace viruses,
winged protozoans:
for the infinite,
intricate shapes
of sub-microscopic
living things.

For algae spores
and fungus spores,
bonded by vital
mutual genetic cooperation,
spreading their
inseparable lives
from equator to pole.

My hand, my arm,
make sweeping circles.
Dust climbs the ladder of light.
For this infernal, endless chore,
for these eternal seeds of rain:
Thank you. For dust.

ROBERT HERRICK
(1591–1674)

Grace for a Child

Here a little child I stand
Heaving up my either hand;
Cold as paddocks though they be,
Here I lift them up to thee,
For a benison to fall
On our meat and on us all. Amen.

HENRY WADSWORTH LONGFELLOW
(1807–1882)

The Harvest Moon

It is the Harvest Moon! On gilded vanes
   And roofs of villages, on woodland crests
   And their aerial neighborhoods of nests
   Deserted, on the curtained window-panes
Of rooms where children sleep, on country lanes
   And harvest-fields, its mystic splendor rests!
   Gone are the birds that were our summer guests,
   With the last sheaves return the laboring wains!
All things are symbols: the external shows
   Of Nature have their image in the mind,
   As flowers and fruits and falling of the leaves;
The song-birds leave us at the summer's close,
   Only the empty nests are left behind,
   And pipings of the quail among the sheaves.

AMY LEVY
(1861–1889)

At a Dinner Party

With fruit and flowers the board is deckt,
  The wine and laughter flow;
I'll not complain—could one expect
  So dull a world to know?

You look across the fruit and flowers,
  My glance your glances find.—
It is our secret, only ours,
  Since all the world is blind.

EMILY DICKINSON
(1830–1886)

One Day is there
of the Series (814)

One Day is there of the Series
Termed Thanksgiving Day.
Celebrated part at Table
Part in Memory.

Neither Patriarch nor Pussy
I dissect the Play
Seems it to my Hooded thinking
Reflex Holiday.

Had there been no sharp Subtraction
From the early Sum—
Not an Acre or a Caption
Where was once a Room—

Not a Mention, whose small Pebble
Wrinkled any Sea,
Unto Such, were such Assembly
'Twere Thanksgiving Day

ALBERTO RÍOS
(1952–)

When Giving Is All We Have

One river gives
Its journey to the next.

We give because someone gave to us.
We give because nobody gave to us.

We give because giving has changed us.
We give because giving could have changed us.

We have been better for it,
We have been wounded by it—

Giving has many faces: It is loud and quiet,
Big, though small, diamond in wood-nails.

Its story is old, the plot worn and the pages too,
But we read this book, anyway, over and again:

Giving is, first and every time, hand to hand,
Mine to yours, yours to mine.

You gave me blue and I gave you yellow.
Together we are simple green. You gave me

What you did not have, and I gave you
What I had to give—together, we made

Something greater from the difference.

CARL SANDBURG
(1878–1967)

Fire Dreams

(Written to be read aloud, if so be, Thanksgiving Day)

I remember here by the fire,
In the flickering reds and saffrons,
They came in a ramshackle tub,
Pilgrims in tall hats,
Pilgrims of iron jaws,
Drifting by weeks on beaten seas,
And the random chapters say
They were glad and sang to God.

And so
Since the iron-jawed men sat down
And said, "Thanks, O God,"
For life and soup and a little less
Than a hobo handout to-day,
Since gray winds blew gray patterns of sleet on Plymouth Rock,
Since the iron-jawed men sang "Thanks, O God,"
You and I, O Child of the West,
Remember more than ever
November and the hunter's moon,
November and the yellow-spotted hills.

And so
In the name of the iron-jawed men
I will stand up and say yes till the finish is come and gone.
God of all broken hearts, empty hands, sleeping soldiers,
God of all star-flung beaches of night sky,
I and my love-child stand up together to-day and sing: "Thanks, O God."

CHRISTOPHER GILBERT
(1949–2007)

On the Way Back Home

It's a different world
now that we've found a doe dead, against
a late fall background crystalled with frost, steaming
still, in the middle of the two-lane as it goes
where the forest starts going west of the city,
while the feeling is as we hover hushed over her,
everything dark except for the florescent white
flashlight beam sheeming back from the various sleek
facets of her sad and useless beauty, she was
one of us though more like a fallen star
the three of us had wandered to witness,
her otherness a light from her eyes facing up
went nowhere, was all there on itself
existing as an end in itself, instructive so
we couldn't follow it but were compelled—
like refugees awaiting our turns to be
an absence happening, a promising effect—
to turn our gaze onto our absent selves,
to turn our attention into a thing
to inspect, and from this focus point, go out
wandering in our various directions.

CARL ADAMSHICK
(1969–)

Everything That Happens Can Be Called Aging

I have more love than ever.
Our kids have kids soon to have kids.
I need them. I need everyone
to come over to the house,
sleep on the floor, on the couches
in the front room. I need noise,
too many people in too small a space,
I need dancing, the spilling of drinks,
the loud pronouncements
over music, the verbal sparring,
the broken dishes, the wealth.
I need it all flying apart.
My friends to slam against me,
to hold me, to say they love me.
I need mornings to ask for favors
and forgiveness. I need to give,
have all my emotions rattled,
my family to be greedy,
to keep coming, to keep asking
and taking. I need no resolution,
just the constant turmoil of living.
Give me the bottom of the river,
all the unadorned, unfinished,
unpraised moments, one good turn
on the luxuriant wheel.

BEN KOPEL
(1983–)

What Is True

one must be one
to ever be two

and if you
were a day
I'd find a way

to live
through you

PABLO MEDINA
(1948–)

At the Blue Note

for Karen Bentivenga

Sometimes in the heat of the snow
you want to cry out

for pleasure or pain like a bell.
And you wind up holding each other,

listening to the in-between
despite the abyss at the edge of the table.

Hell. Mulgrew Miller plays like a big
bad spider, hands on fire, the piano

trembling like crystal,
the taste and smell of a forest under water.

The bartender made us a drink
with butterfly wings and electric wire.

Bitter cold outside, big silence,
a whale growing inside us.

NOELLE KOCOT
(1969–)

Happiness

Our ancestors in the earth are not
Ashamed of us. The strong smell
Of dirt, the delirious rabbits, the
Clocks are all disappearing. A

Prehistoric gift acquires the smell
Of salt. I grasp onto winter's tail.
Some water plants are lying around.
Smell & taste, I have had good

Luck in love. The slippery roads,
The capricious numbers on a blazing
Road, meet me at the forest's edge
Where we can go with our legs

Lopped off, strangers to the clean
Teeth and tongue of outward happiness.

JENNY BROWNE
(1971–)

Love Letter to a Stranger

Tell us of a bypassed heart beating in 12C,
how the woman holds a stranger's hand
to the battery sewn in beneath her collarbone,
and says feel this. Tell us of the man's ear
listening across the aisle, hugging itself,
a fist long since blistered by blaze.
Outside, morning sun buckling up.
Inside, twitching bonesacks of bat, birdsong
erupting as light cracks the far jungle canopy.
Ten thousand feet below ours, a grey cat
tongues the morning's butter left out to soft.
Last night we broke open the sweet folds
around two paper fortunes. One said variety.
One said caution. The woman in 12C would hold that
her heart needs its hidden spark, but the man shows
how some live the rest of their lives with half a face
remembering its before expression. Who was it
that said our souls know one another
by smell, like horses?

December

New Stanzas for
Amazing Grace

I dreamed I dwelled in a homeless place
Where I was lost alone
Folk looked right through me into space
And passed with eyes of stone

O homeless hand on many a street
Accept this change from me
A friendly smile or word is sweet
As fearless charity

Woe workingman who hears the cry
And cannot spare a dime
Nor look into a homeless eye
Afraid to give the time

So rich or poor no gold to talk
A smile on your face
The homeless ones where you may walk
Receive amazing grace

I dreamed I dwelled in a homeless place
Where I was lost alone
Folk looked right through me into space
And passed with eyes of stone

ALICIA OSTRIKER
(1937–)

from psalm

I am not lyric any more
I will not play the harp
for your pleasure

I will not make a joyful
noise to you, neither
will I lament

for I know you drink
lamentation, too,
like wine

so I dully repeat
you hurt me
I hate you

I pull my eyes away from the hills
I will not kill for you
I will never love you again

unless you ask me

LIZETTE WOODWORTH REESE
(1856–1935)

Old Houses

Old loveliness, set in the country wind,
Or down some vain town road the careless tread,
Like hush of candles lighted for the dead,
That look of yours, half seeing and half blind.
Still do you strain at door, but we come not,
The little maids, the lads, bone of your bone;
In some sad wise, you keep the dusk alone,
Old loveliness, a many a day forgot.
But no; behind each weather do you pass,
The garnered poignancies of all the springs:
At some girl's belt in Lent the jonquils start;—
But, oh, their like in your old windy grass!
Then are we quick with tears, rememberings;
Once more, once more, are gathered to your heart!

MARIE PONSOT
(1921–)

Testing Gardening

In the garden I watch myself take care
as if I were the garden. I even learn
from experience! Slowly (fair is fair),
I may grow less stupid and learn to turn
error to advantage — though mistakes take
years of uprooting seedlings sprung from seed
dropped a decade ago in error's long wake.
I was right to want you, to sweat, weed,
balance acid soil, shield you from sunscald
early, then prune to make sure the sun you need
found you. For these few spring weeks you're a sprawl
of flowers, you green the summer toward its rest
in fruited autumn. Yet it's winter that's best,

yes, to imagine joy, next. The winter test.

W. S. MERWIN
(1927–)

The New Song

For some time I thought there was time
and that there would always be time
for what I had a mind to do
and what I could imagine
going back to and finding it
as I had found it the first time
but by this time I do not know
what I thought when I thought back then

there is no time yet it grows less
there is the sound of rain at night
arriving unknown in the leaves
once without before or after
then I hear the thrush waking
at daybreak singing the new song

ROBERT HAYDEN
(1913–1980)

Those Winter Sundays

Sundays too my father got up early
and put his clothes on in the blueblack cold,
then with cracked hands that ached
from labor in the weekday weather made
banked fires blaze. No one ever thanked him.

I'd wake and hear the cold splintering, breaking.
When the rooms were warm, he'd call,
and slowly I would rise and dress,
fearing the chronic angers of that house,

Speaking indifferently to him,
who had driven out the cold
and polished my good shoes as well.
What did I know, what did I know
of love's austere and lonely offices?

JOAN LARKIN
(1939–)

The Combo

In barlight alchemized: gold pate, the bellmouth
tenor, liquor trapped in a glass. The e-flat
clarinet chases time, strings shudder,
remembering the hundred tongues. Here comes old
snakeshine, scrolls stored in the well, here comes
the sobbing chazzan. O my lucky uncle,
you've escaped the Czar's army. Thunder
is sweet. Here comes the boink, boink bossa
nova slant of light. Snow-dollars
dissolve on a satin tongue. The river
swells green, concrete trembles, and we
sweat, leaning toward mikes and wires
as the last tune burns down to embers. Ash-
whispers. We were born before we were born.

LINDA GREGG
(1942–)

We Manage Most When
We Manage Small

What things are steadfast? Not the birds.
Not the bride and groom who hurry
in their brevity to reach one another.
The stars do not blow away as we do.
The heavenly things ignite and freeze.
But not as my hair falls before you.
Fragile and momentary, we continue.
Fearing madness in all things huge
and their requiring. Managing as thin light
on water. Managing only greetings
and farewells. We love a little, as the mice
huddle, as the goat leans against my hand.
As the lovers quickening, riding time.
Making safety in the moment. This touching
home goes far. This fishing in the air.

Darkening, Then Brightening

The sky keeps lying to the farmhouse,
lining up its heavy clouds
above the blue table umbrella,
then launching them over the river.
And the day feels hopeless
until it notices a few trees
dropping delicately their white petals
on the grass beside the birdhouse
perched on its wooden post,
the blinking fledglings stuffed inside
like clothes in a tiny suitcase. At first
you wandered lonely through the yard
and it was no help knowing Wordsworth
felt the same, but then Whitman
comforted you a little, and you saw
the grass as uncut hair, yearning
for the product to make it shine.
Now you lie on the couch beneath the skylight,
the sky starting to come clean,
mixing its cocktail of sadness and dazzle,
a deluge and then a digging out
and then enough time for one more
dance or kiss before it starts again,
darkening, then brightening.
You listen to the tall wooden clock
in the kitchen: its pendulum clicks
back and forth all day, and it chimes
with a pure sound, every hour on the hour,
though it always mistakes the hour.

CAROLINE ELIZABETH SARAH NORTON
(1808–1877)

We Have Been
Friends Together

We have been friends together,
    In sunshine and in shade;
Since first beneath the chestnut trees
    In infancy we played.
But coldness dwells within thy heart,
    A cloud is on thy brow;
We have been friends together—
    Shall a light word part us now?

We have been gay together;
    We have laughed at little jests;
For the fount of hope was gushing
    Warm and joyous in our breasts.
But laughter now hath fled thy lip,
    And sullen glooms thy brow;
We have been gay together—
    Shall a light word part us now?

We have been sad together;
    We have wept with bitter tears
O'er the grass-grown graves where slumbered
    The hopes of early years.
The voices which were silent there
    Would bid thee clear thy brow;
We have been sad together—
    Oh, what shall part us now?

YUSEF KOMUNYAKAA
(1947–)

The Smokehouse

In the hickory scent
Among slabs of pork
Glistening with salt,
I played Indian
In a headdress of redbird feathers
& brass buttons
Off my mother's winter coat.
Smoke wove
A thread of fire through meat, into December
& January. The dead weight
Of the place hung around me,
Strung up with sweetgrass.
The hog had been sectioned,
A map scored into skin;
Opened like love,
From snout to tail,
The goodness
No longer true to each bone.
I was a wizard
In that hazy world,
& knew I could cut
Slivers of meat till my heart
Grew more human & flawed.

LINDA GREGERSON
(1950–)

Narrow Flame

Dark still. Twelve degrees below freezing.
>Tremor along
>>the elegant, injured right front

leg of the gelding on the cross-ties. Kneeling
>girl.
>>The undersong of waters as she bathes

the leg in yet more cold. [tongue is broken]
>[god to me]
>>Her hair the color of winter wheat.

JEFFREY MCDANIEL
(1967–)

Jonathan

We are underwater off the coast of Belize.
The water is lit up even though it's dark
as if there are illuminated seashells
scattered on the ocean floor.
We're not wearing oxygen tanks,
yet staying underwater for long stretches.
We are looking for the body of the boy
we lost. Each year he grows a little older.
Last December you opened his knapsack
and stuck in a plastic box of carrots.
Even though we're underwater, we hear
a song playing over a policeman's radio.
He comes to the shoreline to park
and eat midnight sandwiches, his headlights
fanning out across the harbor.
And I hold you close, apple of my closed eye,
red dance of my opened fist.

LOUISE GLÜCK
(1943–)

The Past

Small light in the sky appearing
suddenly between
two pine boughs, their fine needles

now etched onto the radiant surface
and above this
high, feathery heaven—

Smell the air. That is the smell of the white pine,
most intense when the wind blows through it
and the sound it makes equally strange,
like the sound of the wind in a movie—

Shadows moving. The ropes
making the sound they make. What you hear now
will be the sound of the nightingale, *chordata*,
the male bird courting the female—

The ropes shift. The hammock
sways in the wind, tied
firmly between two pine trees.

Smell the air. That is the smell of the white pine.

It is my mother's voice you hear
or is it only the sound the trees make
when the air passes through them

because what sound would it make,
passing through nothing?

JEAN VALENTINE
(1934–)

Friend,

for Adrienne Rich

You came in a dream, yesterday
—the first day we met
you showed me your dark workroom
off the kitchen, your books, your notebooks.

Reading our last, knowing-last letters
—the years of our friendship
reading our poems to each other,
I would start breathing again.

Yesterday, in the afternoon,
more than a year since you died,
some words came into the air.
I looked away a second,
and they were gone,
six lines, just passing through.

SARA TEASDALE
(1884–1933)

The Gift

What can I give you, my lord, my lover,
You who have given the world to me,
Showed me the light and the joy that cover
The wild sweet earth and the restless sea?

All that I have are gifts of your giving—
If I gave them again, you would find them old,
And your soul would weary of always living
Before the mirror my life would hold.

What shall I give you, my lord, my lover?
The gift that breaks the heart in me:
I bid you awake at dawn and discover
I have gone my way and left you free.

STANLEY KUNITZ
(1905–2006)

An Old Cracked Tune

My name is Solomon Levi,
the desert is my home,
my mother's breast was thorny,
and father I had none.

The sands whispered, *Be separate*,
the stones taught me, *Be hard*.
I dance, for the joy of surviving,
on the edge of the road.

26

Your names toll in my dreams.
I pick up tinsel in the street. A nameless god
streaks my hand with blood. I look at the lighted trees
in windows & the spindles of pine tremble
in warm rooms. The flesh of home, silent.
How quiet the bells of heaven must be, cold
with stars who cannot rhyme their brilliance
to our weapons. What rouses our lives each moment?
Nothing but life dares dying. My memory, another obituary.
My memory is a cross. Face down. A whistle in high grass.
A shadow pouring down the sill of calamity.
Your names wake me in the nearly dark hour.
The candles in our windows flicker
where your faces peer in, ask us
questions light cannot answer.

ARTHUR SZE
(1950–)

The Chance

The blue-black mountains are etched
with ice. I drive south in fading light.
The lights of my car set out before
me, and disappear before my very eyes.
And as I approach thirty, the distances
are shorter than I guess? The mind
travels at the speed of light. But for
how many people are the passions
ironwood, ironwood that hardens and hardens?
Take the ex-musician, insurance salesman,
who sells himself a policy on his own life;
or the magician who has himself locked
in a chest and thrown into the sea,
only to discover he is caught in his own chains.
I want a passion that grows and grows.
To feel, think, act, and be defined
by your actions, thoughts, feelings.
As in the bones of a hand in an X ray,
I want the clear white light to work
against the fuzzy blurred edges of the darkness:
even if the darkness precedes and follows
us, we have a chance, briefly, to shine.

YONA HARVEY
(1974–)

The Subject of Retreat

Your black coat is a door
in the storm. The snow
we don't mention
clings to your boots & powders
& puffs. & poof. Goes.
Dust of the fallen. Right here
at home. The ache
of someone gone-missing. Walk it off
like a misspoken word.
Mound of snow. Closed door.
I could open it.

Or maybe just, you know—
brush it off.

Then what? The snow
on the other side. The sound
of what I know & your, *no*, inside it.

MARK STRAND
(1934–2014)

The Coming of Light

Even this late it happens:
the coming of love, the coming of light.
You wake and the candles are lit as if by themselves,
stars gather, dreams pour into your pillows,
sending up warm bouquets of air.
Even this late the bones of the body shine
and tomorrow's dust flares into breath.

Tanner's *Annunciation*

Gabriel disembodied,
pure column of light.

Humble Mary, receiving the word
that the baby she carries is God's.

Not good news, not news, even,
but rather the rightly enormous word,

Annunciation. She knew
they were chosen. She knew

he would suffer, as the chosen child
always suffers. Perhaps she knew

the dearest wish, mercy,
would be ever-inchoate,

like Gabriel: light that carries
possibility, illuminates,

but that can promise nothing but itself.

EMILY DICKINSON
(1830–1886)

The Savior must have been (1487)

The Savior must have been
A docile Gentleman—
To come so far so cold a Day
For little Fellowmen—

The Road to Bethlehem
Since He and I were Boys
Was leveled, but for that 'twould be
A rugged Billion Miles—

THOMAS HARDY
(1840–1928)

The Oxen

Christmas Eve, and twelve of the clock.
  'Now they are all on their knees,'
An elder said as we sat in a flock
  By the embers in hearthside ease.

We pictured the meek mild creatures where
  They dwelt in their strawy pen,
Nor did it occur to one of us there
  To doubt they were kneeling then.

So fair a fancy few would weave
  In these years! Yet, I feel,
If someone said on Christmas Eve,
  'Come; see the oxen kneel,

In the lonely barton by yonder coomb
  Our childhood used to know,'
I should go with him in the gloom,
  Hoping it might be so.

MEENA ALEXANDER
(1951–)

Night Theater

Snails circle
A shed where a child was born.

She bled into straw—
Who can write this?

Under Arcturus,
Rubble of light:

We have no words
For what is happening—

Still language endures
Celan said

As he stood in a torn
Green coat

Shivering a little,
In a night theater, in Bremen.

CYNTHIA ZARIN
(1959–)

Skating in Harlem, Christmas Day

To Mary Jo Salter

Beyond the ice-bound stones and bucking trees,
past bewildered Mary, the Meer in snow,
two skating rinks and two black crooked paths

are a battered pair of reading glasses
scratched by the skater's multiplying math.
Beset, I play this game of tic-tac-toe.

Divide, subtract. Who can tell if love surpasses?
Two noughts we've learned make one astonished O—
a hectic night of goats and compasses.

Folly tells the truth by what it's not—
one X equals a fall I'd not forgo.
Are ice and fire the integers we've got?

Skating backwards tells another story—
the risky star above the freezing town,
a way to walk on water and not drown.

MARY SZYBIST
(1970–)

In Tennessee I Found a Firefly

Flashing in the grass; the mouth of a spider clung
    to the dark of it: the legs of the spider
held the tucked wings close,
    held the abdomen still in the midst of calling
with thrusts of phosphorescent light—

When I am tired of being human, I try to remember
    the two stuck together like burrs. I try to place them
central in my mind where everything else must
    surround them, must see the burr and the barb of them.
There is courtship, and there is hunger. I suppose
    there are grips from which even angels cannot fly.
Even imagined ones. *Luciferin, luciferase.*
    When I am tired of only touching,
I have my mouth to try to tell you
    what, in your arms, is not erased.

JANE KENYON
(1947–1995)

Taking Down the Tree

"Give me some light!" cries Hamlet's
uncle midway through the murder
of Gonzago. "Light! Light!" cry scattering
courtesans. Here, as in Denmark,
it's dark at four, and even the moon
shines with only half a heart.

The ornaments go down into the box:
the silver spaniel, *My Darling*
on its collar, from Mother's childhood
in Illinois; the balsa jumping jack
my brother and I fought over,
pulling limb from limb. Mother
drew it together again with thread
while I watched, feeling depraved
at the age of ten.

With something more than caution
I handle them, and the lights, with their
tin star-shaped reflectors, brought along
from house to house, their pasteboard
toy suitcase increasingly flimsy.
Tick, tick, the desiccated needles drop.

By suppertime all that remains is the scent
of balsam fir. If it's darkness
we're having, let it be extravagant.

RUTH ELLEN KOCHER
(1965–)

Another Myth

Days are most difficult, sky not quite blue
but yielding to the dark expansion
that's brought stars into being.
I'm only a woman alone without women,
confused by these restraints of naming:
rose bud, red clay, gazelle or azalea
unbound to bloom or bound
into a bloom of wind. In my other valley,
a serpent silked over rocks to find me,
his tongue a riddle of slick muscle
and sureness like Adam's as he sang
names into the empty mouths of animals.
Left to a world, new again,
I have smothered a fire,
swallowed the night.

DYLAN THOMAS
(1914–1953)

Do Not Go Gentle into That Good Night

Do not go gentle into that good night,
Old age should burn and rave at close of day;
Rage, rage against the dying of the light.

Though wise men at their end know dark is right,
Because their words had forked no lightning they
Do not go gentle into that good night.

Good men, the last wave by, crying how bright
Their frail deeds might have danced in a green bay,
Rage, rage against the dying of the light.

Wild men who caught and sang the sun in flight,
And learn, too late, they grieved it on its way,
Do not go gentle into that good night.

Grave men, near death, who see with blinding sight
Blind eyes could blaze like meteors and be gay,
Rage, rage against the dying of the light.

And you, my father, there on the sad height,
Curse, bless, me now with your fierce tears, I pray.
Do not go gentle into that good night.
Rage, rage against the dying of the light.

Recovery

For Dugald

A last love,
proper in conclusion,
should snip the wings,
forbidding further flight.

But I, now,
reft of that confusion,
am lifted up
and speeding toward the light.

Permissions

Poet Index

Subject Index

ABOUT THE ACADEMY OF AMERICAN POETS

The Academy of American Poets is the largest membership-based nonprofit organization that fosters an appreciation for contemporary poetry and supports American poets. For more than three decades, the Academy of American Poets has connected millions of people to great poetry through programs such as Poem-a-Day, a daily digital poetry publication series; National Poetry Month, the largest literary celebration in the world; Poets.org, the Academy's popular website; *American Poets*, a biannual literary journal; and an annual series of poetry readings and special events. Since its founding, the Academy of American Poets has awarded more money to poets than any other organization.

Poem-a-Day: 365 Poems for Every Occasion was inspired by the Academy of American Poets' Poem-a-Day series, which features more than two hundred new, previously unpublished poems by today's talented poets each year. On weekdays, poems are accompanied by exclusive commentary by the poets. The series highlights classic poems on weekends. Launched in 2006, Poem-a-Day is now distributed via email, web, and social media to more than 300,000 readers free of charge and is available for syndication by King Features.

Visit Poets.org for more information about the Academy of American Poets and to sign up for Poem-a-Day.